The Muse Strikes Back

A POETIC RESPONSE BY WOMEN TO MEN

edited by Katherine McAlpine & Gail White

Story Line Press   1997

Published by Story Line Press, Inc.,
Three Oaks Farm, Brownsville, OR 97327

This publication was made possible thanks in part to the generous support
of the Nicholas Roerich Museum, the Andrew W. Mellon Foundation,
the Eric Mathieu King Fund, the Charles Schwab Corporation Foundation,
and our individual contributors.

Book design by Chiquita Babb

Library of Congress Cataloging-in-Publication Data
The muse strikes back : a poetic response by women to men / edited by
  Katherine McAlpine and Gail White.
       p.   cm.
    ISBN 1-885266-49-9
       1. American poetry—Women authors. 2. Man-woman relationships—
Poetry. 3. English poetry—Women authors. 4. Poetry—Men authors—
Poetry. 5. Feminism—Poetry. 6. Poetics—Poetry. 7. Women—
Poetry. I. McAlpine, Katherine, 1948–   . II. White, Gail, 1945–   .
PS589.M87   1997
811.008'09287—dc21   97-25390
                                                                     CIP

Contents

The Latin Poets

Medieval and Renaissance Poets

The Seventeenth-Century Poets

The Nineteenth-Century Poets

Introduction

"A WOMAN WHO concerns herself with poetry," writes Robert Graves in *The White Goddess*, "should. . .be a silent Muse and inspire the poets by her womanly presence. . . . She should be the visible moon: impartial, loving, severe, wise." More recently, in a book of advice for writers by a popular male author, almost all the several dozen cartoons show a male writer at work, while women are most commonly depicted as voluptuous, gauzily clad Muses—with wings and lyres, no less—hovering sweetly above his head.

Old archetypes certainly die hard.

The archetype of the Muse does not work very well when one attempts to reverse the traditional genders (just try to visualize, without snickering, a woman writer at her desk while some hunk of celestial beefcake floats nearby). For one thing, few men have been willing—and with good reason—to assume the role of silent, impartial satellite. For another, the concept of creative power as dwelling in an entity outside oneself—a fickle Other who must be wooed into dispensing inspirational favors—is one that the creative woman may find psychologically difficult, if not downright invalid.

In studying the male poetic canon, which until recently was almost the entire poetic canon, we find few female characters with identities, minds, and agendas of their own, few flesh-and-blood heroines like Chaucer's Wife of Bath. Dante's Beatrice, Wordsworth's Lucy, and Poe's Annabel Lee are all misty, distant moons, passively reflecting the male poet's vision. (It seems to help a lot if the lady's dead.) Keats's Belle Dame sans Merci is only the dark side of the archetype: the dangerous (but equally silent) seductress who exists to lure men to their doom. Lesbia, Ann Donne, Marvell's Coy Mistress, Elizabeth Siddal Rossetti, and the recipient of Shelley's "To__" don't get to tell their own sides of the stories.

In this volume, however, they do. Here Sara Teasdale gives voice to Beatrice, Annie Finch and D.A. Prince to the Coy Mistress, Dorothy Parker to Lesbia, Karen Donnelly and Mary Holtby to Ann Donne, while other women retell classical poetry and biblical stories from the female perspective. In other selections, women poets respond to the work of men by challenging their assumptions and deflating their pretensions: see Kathleen Iddings's reply to Williams and Debra Pennington's to Yeats, Diane Engle's spoof of

Ashbery and Barbara Harr's parody of Bly, Carolyn Kizer's impassioned argument with Juvenal and Wendy Cope's wickedly funny "Waste Land Limericks." Here, too, are Phyllis McGinley and Lady Mary Wortley Montagu—the former sometimes dismissed as a "housewife poet," the latter slandered by Pope as a "whore"— defying stereotypes at their sly, satiric best.

Poets of both sexes, in every culture and era, have traditionally written many poems to or about other poets: arguing, paying homage, lampooning, or otherwise drawing inspiration from their work. The impulse is part literary, part social. No writer develops in a vacuum; we all learn, initially, by studying and emulating our predecessors (though we may later rebel against them and disown their influence). As we acquire skill and confidence, we begin to seek a more creative and assertive relationship with both the past and our peers. By addressing other poets in verse, we can engage them in conversation. We can talk to the dead—or to contemporaries we might never actually meet. In doing so, we connect ourselves to the literary continuum and claim our place on the family tree.

Women poets have historically had a less visible and less influential position in that continuum. Yet precisely because of their relative isolation, the need to establish a sense of literary kinship has, perhaps, been all the more intense. In addition, the woman poet's relationship to her heritage has been complicated by the probability that her artistic mentors and exemplars have been men, while some viewpoints expressed in their work may have felt alien to her own experience and sensibilities. For these reasons, women's poetic responses to male poets struck us as an especially intriguing subject for an anthology.

The Muse Strikes Back has been a journey of discovery for its editors. When we first began work on the project, we didn't know what we'd find, for such a collection, to our knowledge, had never been done before. We wondered if we could locate enough poems for a slender volume. What we found was a venerable and ongoing tradition of spirited female backtalk. Anne Bradstreet, Susanna Zeidler, Emilia Lanier, the Countess of Winchilsea, Amy Lowell, Louise Bogan, and other distinguished predecessors spoke out with vigor and wit. Submissions from contemporary women were so numerous that space requirements prevented us from including many well-written and interesting poems. To the poets who do not appear in these pages, as well as those who do, we express our heartfelt gratitude.

We'd hoped for variety, and that is definitely what we got. The poems here address more than ninety male poets from Homer to the present, several biblical accounts that we assume to be of male origin, and a few contemporary poets who must, for reasons that will be obvious, remain anonymous. The selections range in tone from wryly amused to fiercely outraged. (Milton, among all the submissions received, came in for some of the sternest rebukes, while Marvell, another popular subject, elicited more good-humored debate.) For balance, we have also included several tributes to male poets, among them Marilyn Hacker's "Elevens" (for James Wright), Rhina P. Espaillat's "For Robert Frost," and Judith Bishop's "Brodsky." The forms employed are diverse: sonnet, ottava rima, villanelle, sapphics, sestina, pantoum, triolet, limerick, epigram, rhymed couplets, quatrains, triplets, blank verse, free verse, and nonce forms.

Our research yielded some surprises that we're delighted to share: worthy but seldom-anthologized poems by Amy Lowell, Sara Teasdale, and H.D.; a satire in rhymed quatrains by Erica Jong; a defense of Eve by Emilia Lanier, whom some scholars believe to have been Shakespeare's Dark Lady; a reply to Swift's "The Lady's Dressing-Room" by an anonymous 18th-century woman; a poem by Esther Johnson, Swift's "Stella" herself. A number of the contemporary poems are appearing in print for the first time, having been written especially for this volume.

In order to make the book as reader-friendly as possible—for both poets and non-poets, for teachers and students of Women's Studies and general Literature courses—we have provided brief explanatory notes in which we name the poem addressed when this is not specified in title, epigraph, or text. Thus, readers who may not be familiar with any referent poem can, if they wish, easily locate it for comparison. (Most of these referent poems are widely available in textbooks, other anthologies, and collected works.) We hope that teachers will encourage their students to "compare and contrast," and that young poets of both sexes may be inspired to try reply poems of their own. Some of our notes also give background information that we felt would enhance readers' appreciation of the work. We have retained British/Canadian spellings where they were used, while in some cases Americanizing the punctuation.

Finally, *The Muse* must acknowledge some generous women *and* men for their contributions to the project. John Mella, editor of *Light,* and Bruce E. Newling brought several of the poems in this volume to our attention. Many contributors referred us to the work of other women poets and cheered us along the way with enthusiastic letters, cards, and phone calls. Dana Gioia provided helpful advice and encouragement. Bruce Bennett graciously gave permission to include his half of a dialogue with Nancy Winters. A. J. Gordon, Kathy Lewis, Elaine Spinney, and Patrick Spinney gave technical assistance. Nanette Gallant, librarian at WCTC Marine Technology Center, Eastport, Maine, cheerfully tracked down books and information that had nothing to do with boats. Gail thanks her husband, Arthur, and Katherine thanks her son, Nathaniel, for their heroic (though not always unflagging) patience and support. And last but certainly not least, Robert McDowell of Story Line Press believed in the book enough to publish it.

Katherine McAlpine
Eastport, Maine

Gail White
Breaux Bridge, Louisiana

Alas! a woman that attempts the pen,
Such an intruder on the rights of men,
Such a presumptuous creature, is esteem'd,
The fault can by no virtue be redeem'd.
They tell us we mistake our sex and way;
Good breeding, fashion, dancing, dressing, play
Are the accomplishments we should desire;
To write, or read, or think, or to inquire
Would cloud our beauty and exhaust our time,
And interrupt the conquests of our prime;
Whilst the dull manage of a servile house
Is held by some our utmost art and use.

. . . . .

And if some one would soar above the rest,
With warmer fancy and ambition press'd,
So strong th' opposing faction still appears,
The hopes to thrive can ne'er outweigh the fears.
Be caution'd then, my Muse, and still retir'd;
Nor be despis'd, aiming to be admir'd;
Conscious of wants, still with contracted wing,
To some new friends, and to thy sorrow sing;
For groves of laurel thou wert never meant;
Be dark enough thy shades, and be thou there content.

Anne Finch, Countess of Winchilsea, "The Introduction"

Long afterward, Oedipus, old and blinded, walked the
roads.   He smelled a familiar smell.   It was
the Sphinx.   Oedipus said, "I want to ask one question.
Why didn't I recognize my mother?"   "You gave the
wrong answer," said the Sphinx.   "But that was what
made everything possible," said Oedipus.   "No," she said.
"When I asked, What walks on four legs in the morning,
two at noon, and three in the evening, you answered,
Man.   You didn't say anything about woman."
"When you say Man," said Oedipus, "you include women
too. Everyone knows that."   She said, "That's what
you think."

Muriel Rukeyser, "Myth"

The Hebrew Bible

Eves Apologie

Till now your indiscretion sets us free
And makes our former fault much less appeare;
Our Mother *Eve,* who tasted of the Tree,
Giving to *Adam* what shee held most deare,
Was simply good, and had no powre to see,
The after-comming harme did not appeare:
      The subtile Serpent that our Sex betraide,
      Before our fall so sure a plot had laide.

That undiscerning Ignorance perceav'd
No guile, or craft that was by him intended;
For had she knowne, of what we were bereav'd,
To his request she had not condiscended.
But she (poor soule) by cunning was deceav'd,
No hurt therein her harmlesse heart intended:
      For she alleadg'd God's word, which he denies,
      That they should die, but even as Gods, be wise.

But surely *Adam* can not be excusde,
Her fault though great, yet hee was most too blame;
What Weaknesse offered, Strength might have refusde,
Being Lord of all, the greater was his shame:
Although the Serpents craft had her abusde,
Gods holy word ought all his actions frame,
      For he was Lord and King of all the earth,
      Before poore *Eve* had either life or breath.

Who being fram'd by Gods eternall hand
The perfect'st man that ever breath'd on earth;
And from Gods mouth receiv'd that strait command,
The breach whereof he knew was present death:
Yea having powre to rule both Sea and Land,
Yet with one Apple wonne to loose that breath
      Which God had breathed in his beauteous face,
      Bringing us all in danger and disgrace.

And then to lay the fault on Patience backe,
That we (poore women) must endure it all;
We know right well he did discretion lacke,
Beeing not perswaded thereunto at all;
If *Eve* did erre, it was for knowledge sake,
The fruit being faire perswaded him to fall:
        No subtill Serpents falshood did betray him,
        If he would eate it, who had powre to stay him?

Not *Eve,* whose fault was onely too much love,
Which made her give this present to her Deare,
That what shee tasted, he might likewise prove,
Whereby his knowledge might become more cleare;
He never sought her weakenesse to reprove,
With those sharpe words, which he of God did heare:
        Yet Men will boast of knowledge, which he tooke
        From *Eves* fair hand, as from a learned Booke.

If any Evill did in her remaine,
Beeing made of him, he was the ground of all;
If one of many Worlds could lay a staine
Upon our Sexe, and worke so great a fall
To wretched Man, by Satans subtill traine;
What will so fowle a fault amongst you all?
        Her weakenesse did the Serpents words obay,
        But you in malice Gods deare Sonne betray.

Whom, if unjustly you condemne to die,
Her sinne was small, to what you doe commit:
All mortal sinnes that doe for vengeance crie,
Are not to be compared unto it:
If many worlds would altogether trie,
By all their sinnes the wrath of God to get;
        This sinne of yours, surmounts them all as farre
        As doth the Sunne, another little starre.

Then let us have our Libertie againe,
And challendge to your selves no Sov'raigntie;

You came not in the world without our paine,
Make that a barre against your crueltie;
Your fault being greater, why should you disdaine
Our being equals, free from tyranny?
    If one weake woman simply did offend,
    This sinne of yours, hath no excuse, nor end.

Emilia Lanier

Lilith*

Some say Adam reared me from the beasts.
He, tired of coupling with them,
mortared an elixir of earth and berries,
potpourried sage for brows,
olive and ash for eyes.

I told him I could see
future and past, tongue
from which I whisper,
a melody of Valerian,
a power to make him sleep.

He did not know what he was creating;
a woman who desires to be God
while she fucks; I refuse his man-grunts,
his shaft entering from above.
I bite his ear, when he comes from below,
a cherry-blood sweetness.

Some say God was jealous; true,
God had me, God thought my aroma crude.
Fleeing, I seduced Satan, who gave me
children, a hundredfold each day.

Now God's covetous breath is pleading me back;
how can I abandon my children from Him?
For this God names me Succubus,
and my daughters, the Lilium, men and monks
will fear as their wet dreams.

Catherine Martin

*There is only one brief mention of Lilith in the Bible, but her story has survived in Jewish folk-
lore and the Gnostic Gospels. She was the first wife of Adam, created equally with him and cast
out of Eden for her refusal to submit to male dominance. Legend portrays her as an evil spirit,
mother of demons, destroyer of human children, and temptress of men. In the book of *Isaiah*
her name is translated as either "screech owl" or "night monster." According to Merlin Stone in
When God Was a Woman, earlier Sumerian references to Lilith associate her with Goddess-worship.

Noah's Daughter

> Fanciful rabbinic expansions of the Genesis stories were still being
> made in the Middle Ages: answers to such questions by intelligent
> students as— "How was the Ark lighted? How were the animals
> fed? Was there a Phoenix on board?"
> —Robert Graves and Raphael Patai, *Hebrew Myths: the Book of Genesis*

Good questions.
I can answer them
(though you didn't ask me).
Most of the mythical beasts—
the griffin   the Phoenix   the dragon   the centaur—
sailed behind us in a smaller boat.
It was built of imaginary boards
(Father's idea, of course).
The unicorn was tied in back, by its horn.
The sea serpent, naturally, floated underneath.

How were the animals fed?
By all of us—but mostly Mother.

I see her in the tiny, sweaty kitchen
chopping up pieces of seaweed,
making soup out of salt water and discarded shells.
(Meat was forbidden, of course.)
A spider monkey hung by its tail over an improvised stove.
A large red parrot perched on her shoulder.
I sat on the floor, absorbed,
feeding seaweed scraps to the goat.

My mother spoke animal language.
Not all the dialects—just a few.
Leopard and llama were her specialties.
She could also hoot like an owl,
growl like a bear.
My father and brothers marched through the rooms,
pretending they didn't hear.

Sometimes she hung over the deck.
The ocean spoke to her.
It was a violin   a lost child   a lover,
seductive. I knew what it was saying.

Once she leaned over too far, started to sway to its message.
I yelled and held down her ankles.
She said, "Go find your father.
Isn't it feeding time?"

How was the Ark lighted?
It wasn't. It was a dark, musty cave.
At night I'd crawl in on my mother's side of the bunk.
She'd sing songs to me in her throat.
I made her tell me stories:
"Someday we'll get back to land
and we'll have a little house
and you'll have a little room painted peach or apricot.
All the animals will be plush, and won't need feeding.
We'll make sugar cookies and cocoa and be like other people.
The ocean will be very far away."

Beside us, Father snored.
She held me. Her heart beat along with the ocean's.
At these times,
the dark Ark felt safe.
At these times,
I wanted the forty days to go on forever.

Enid Dame

Lot's Wife*

> And Lot's wife looked back
> and became a pillar of salt.

And the just man followed God's ambassador here,
Huge and bright against the mountain black.
But alarm spoke loudly in the woman's ear:
It's not too late, you can still look back

At red-towered Sodom where you were born,
At the square where you sang, where you sat to spin,
At the window of the high house, forlorn,
Where you bore your beloved husband children.

She looked,—deadly pain found the fault,
Her eyes couldn't see if they saw or not;
And her body became translucent salt,
Her lively feet were rooted to the spot.

She's seen as a kind of loss and yet
Who will grieve for this woman, cry for his wife?
My heart alone will never forget:
For a single look, she gave up her life.

Anna Akhmatova
translated by Lyn Coffin

*See *Genesis* 13:1-12.

Dina's Happy Ending

According to one commentary, Dina—who was raped by
Schechem—eventually married Job. It was felt that these two in-
nocent sufferers deserved a happy ending. See Graves and Patai,
Hebrew Myths: the Book of Genesis.

And so I married
the man called Job.
Why not? It seemed right.
We did have a lot in common.
Long pain had rubbed down his edges.
He didn't expect too much:
no thrilling off-center scenarios,
no rants about pride and revenge,
no loud dissertations
on womanhood manhood and God.
No theories at all, I think.
Yes, he was easy to live with.

Love? Are you serious?
Neither of us needed love.
We kept a quiet house.

When he died, though, I cried
a few tears, like small stones.
And all the women came round.
They hugged me,
brewed tea, offered spongecake,
said, "Darling, at least
you had a few good years with him."

I didn't answer.
Their perfume was comforting.

One, young, the youngest of all
with ardent black hair, shining eyes,
grabbed up my hand: "Oh, Aunt Dina,

what a terrific story!
I adore happy endings."

That night in bed, I broke into laughter:
weird, wild, glass-cracking gusts.
I think I laughed half the night.
God, it felt good.

Enid Dame

Miriam*

> When a man goes up to the Summit of Carmel and espies a kind
> of sieve in the Sea of Tiberius, that is Miriam's well.
> —*Legends from the Talmud and Midrash*

She who could see the light of days to come
She who shaped her words into a holy verse
She who was a gracious daughter and sister
She who eased the pains of women in labor
She who was there for women in their sorrow
She who was there for women in their joy
She who led them in their dance and song
She who was there to wipe the orphan's tears
She whose well made wastelands grow figs and vines
She whose days were full, whose nights were empty
She whom the Almighty never made a house
She who, alone of the two who sinned, was cursed
Given no mount for a rest, she lies
Unlamented in the wilderness of Zin

Yala Korwin

*Miriam, mentioned in the books of *Exodus* (Chapter 15) and *Numbers* (Chapter 12), was a
prophetess and the elder sister of Moses and Aaron.

Jael's Poem*

yes
I did it beat
the nail in hard
felt skull crack
like a wineglass crushed
beneath a bridegroom's heel

I didn't hate him
I didn't know him

you understand: I come from
a peculiar people
our men thank god each morning
they aren't women

I used to run in secret
outside the village
and beg my father's god
to make me strong and different

from my gentle mother
who couldn't wring
a chicken's neck

from my sweet-faced sister.
Her screams assaulted
the sleeping village
the night the strange men caught her.
She never married.

but mother told me:
You need a husband.
Heber the Kenite
is not so bad.

and father said:
You're lucky.
You could do worse.

for years I slept
beside a stranger
who grunted and ignored me
one night
another stranger
found my tent

he said: I'm tired
I've lost more than a battle
or a reputation.
he said: I know you're kind
you'll take me in you've got
a mother's face your breasts
are comforting please
let me suckle

of course I said of course
my lord come closer

and reached and found the nail
inside my pocket

and at his look
of sheer amazement I
felt exultation rise
like mercury
inside me

and so I pushed
his light out broke
their sixth commandment

they called him
enemy

and so
they call me
heroine

a Jew at last
although a woman

and a killer

and everyone is pleased
except my husband
he comes home later now
and sleeps
with one eye open

Enid Dame

*See *Judges* 4:17-22.

Not a Voice

> . . .whatsoever cometh forth of the doors of my house to meet
> me. . .I will offer it up for a burnt offering.
>
> —*Judges* 11:32

Clad in festive robes
timbrels in her hands
she dances towards her father
with joyful innocence

Nameless for eternity
accessory to the victor
a virgin sacrificed
in burnt-offering

No council of elders
no curb of prohibition
grounded on Mount Moriah
silence of heavens

No angel to restrain
the murderous arm
not a ram to redeem
a mere girl

Yala Korwin

Abigail

> David said to Abigail. . . "Blessed be your good sense, and blessed
> be you, who have kept me today from bloodguilt and from aveng-
> ing myself by my own hand!"
>
> —1 *Samuel* 25: 32-33

I care for him, although he is a fool.
But when old Nabal turned the king away
and felt so smug, I nearly blew my cool.
I had to act, or there'd be hell to pay.
I packed the wine, the raisins, and the bread,
some sheep prepared for roasting and some grain,
and sent the young men with the mules ahead
in secret. Nabal hasn't got a brain
for politics. He can't help feeling proud
of what he owns.
                    I am this rich man's wife.
I'd rather bear his child than weave his shroud,
so I'll go plead with David for his life,
and reason with the sot when I get back.
But my guess is he'll have a heart attack!

Barbara Loots

Bathsheba: Looking Forward, Looking Back*

It wasn't God who made honky-tonk angels.
                              —Kitty Wells

It was my habit when my husband
was away waging wars to ascend
to the peace of the rooftop at dusk
and bathe my skin in rosewater and myrrh.

I assumed myself alone and loved
imagining the evening I would gaze
toward the sunset and see Uriah riding
home in a cloud of dust and glory.

How was I to know a king would stoop
to take his leisure as a spy, a voyeur
too long accustomed to possessions?
When he summoned, I obeyed. Refusal

I feared would be treason. But for a woman
submission's often judged both virtue
and transgression. Faithful subject.
Faithful wife. Either way I stood condemned.

My husband's blood stained David's hands,
but the child struck down to atone was also mine.
No child, not even Solomon in all his splendor,
ever replaced the one who died in my arms.

Years later I watched David mourn for Absalom—
his treacherous son—but he seemed to forget
our first-born's innocence before his skin had grown cold.
I wondered then if the heart he bore was human.

Oh, but when he sang! I admit my own heart
melted when his tongue filled my ear
with lamentations and praises, when the iron hand
he ruled with stroked his lyre strings

soft as feathers. Me, he never touched
that way again, coming to me more to restake
a claim than to find—much less to give—
comfort or pleasure. Small wonder

in old age his own flesh turned ice—
cold as the shoulder he'd given so many
who had come to him offering love.
His pride earned him impotence.

How pathetic he was with that Shunamite
he commanded to his deathbed, too blind
to see her cringe each time he insisted
on trying. And failed. She was too young

to have heard the songs of his youth.
To be seduced by his cunning with giants
or how he'd worked his way up
from a sheep pen into a palace.

Sometimes I wish I'd known him then.
That I'd been the one to spy from a rooftop
on a boy, half-naked, serenading his flock.
But what use are such wishes to a woman my age?

What does a queen know of shepherds?
Except that night after night I dream
of my children's children and see looming
in their future a stable instead of a throne.

There are three strange men in this dream
and a girl who looks a lot like me.
She bows to the words of a beckoning dove.
The wind fills with the rush of his wings.

And then I wake up. Trembling in light.

Grace Bauer

Kohl

> When Jehu came to Jezebel, Jezebel heard of it; and she painted
> her eyes, and adorned her head, and looked out of the window.
> And as Jehu entered the gate, she said, "Is it peace, you Zimiri,
> murderer of your master?" And he lifted up his face to the win-
> dow, and said. . ."Throw her down." So they threw her down; and
> some of her blood spattered on the wall and on the horses, and
> they trampled on her. —2 *Kings* 9: 30-33

> She piled up stones pretending they were home.
> —"Kairos and Logos," W.H. Auden

There was a time before I called myself
a woman when I played about my father's
sun lit temple, his temple gong my mirror
of who I was. I had no use for paint
or power—these clawed hands were pretty pieces.
I piled up stones pretending they were home.

The god of rain and thunder was his mirror
of how one ought to mount the clouds of self
with neither shame nor pity. Baal was peace-
ful after the rains—as was my incensed father.
I piled up stones pretending they were home.
He oiled Baal's darkened cedar hide for paint.

Between the desert and the sea the piece
that fit was me. My purple sea this mirror:
I piled up stones pretending they were home,
mounted the cloudy throne of self.
I gave commands, saw through my regal painted
eyes 800 priests multiplying father.

They piled up stones pretending they were home,
assembled my cedar Baal—each piece
of horn and leg and phallus painted
green, purple, gold—my dear Phoenician mirror
of what the desert looked like after father
thunder had sown the land with scattered self.

What color is these Jews' invisible paint?
They pile up stones pretending they are home
to the god I Am pretending he is father
in the land of Canaan. Where is their peace?
Why did they choose our cedar for themselves,
adorning their false temple, their mirror

of what they say their creator-father
made? Their laws are clever curses; they paint
their desert with my husband's blood
and pile up stones pretending god is home.
These kohl-edged eyes can see beyond this mirror
the darkening window, my truth in pieces:

I paint my eyes before my father's mirror.
I piled up stones pretending they were home.
Their prophet calls up himself. Is it peace?

Nola Garrett

Esther*

> Even in Persia, in perfumes and bangles and silk stuff, she
> remembered she was a Jew.
> —Maxine Kumin, "Haman's Ears"

Let's face it
(I told my mirror),
I have a talent.

Men see themselves reflected in my eyes
those clever pools
that give them back themselves
but magnified and burnished,
rewritten heroes.
It's something I do well a skill
It isn't Jewish.
It isn't Persian.
I couldn't be like Vashti all joints and angles
her gold eyes striking sparks.
She took a stand. Where did that get her?
I'm standing in her bedroom now. The mirror swallowed her.
I wear her jewels. They glint like tiger eyes.
They suit my coloring.

When uncle came
with his sad news his shabby clothes his sense of duty
(it smelled like ryebread),
I could have said, "Forget it!
I'm not a Jew. My family is Jewish.
I live here, in the palace
with my lush-haired cats my elaborate recipes
and my king
who loves to read
his story in my face.
It's our bedtime ritual our aphrodisiac.
He'll never get enough.

I could have said, "The others?
Those jostling strings of relatives their cardboard suitcases
their garlic breath their gold false teeth
their vulgar jewelry?
Those skinny fiddlers furtive poets sweat-palmed anarchists
toting their packs of leaflets worn instruments injustices
that drop like feathers from goosedown pillows
their darting birds of hands?"

I could have said, "*Mishpocheh,*
you have no claim on me.

I knew you once. Not now.
I've made myself a Queen.
I know how to face the future
my face helped me construct
alone." I could have said that.

But I was good,
a *shayne maydele*.
I smiled at Uncle.
I said, "I'll do my best."
(He smiled back,
a thin-crust smile.)

Then later,
in our private room,
I smiled again.
"Your majesty,
I must confess
I've got a secret...."
He looked up, curious.
A new twist to the story!
I widened my dark eyes
and all the fruit dropped in my hands.
I'll share it. I'm not selfish.
You don't even have to thank me.

But I didn't have to do it.
Always remember that.

Enid Dame

Mishpocheh: family; *shayne maydele:* pretty little girl. Esther, in the book bearing her name, was the wife of the Persian King Ahasuerus. When her cousin Mordecai refused to bow to Haman, the king's counselor, Haman threatened to execute Mordecai and all the captive Jews. Esther interceded with the king on her people's behalf, and Haman himself was later killed. The feast of Purim is celebrated in her honor.

My Song for Solomon

I have drunk the poisoned milk
and breathed the fatal oxygen
and yet live, a ghost among the living.

I have kissed the devil's foot
and sung the angels' songs,
damned woman among the blessed living.

I have neared the end of bed
with an admiring man, and live
quenchless, a ghost, almost, among men.

I wear my gauzy gown, slow sap rising,
still desiring, looking
less tempting, so I undress alone.

Waking from sad sleep, I quake,
the sultry song of Solomon warming
the blood of a ghost among the living.

B.B. Adams

from *Hosea Three*

> When the Lord began to speak through Hosea, the Lord said to
> him, "Go take yourself an adulterous wife. . . ." so he married
> Gomer daughter of Diablaim.
> <div align="right">—<i>Hosea</i> 1: 2-3</div>

Gomer

Am I more than a slippery hole for
you? I have been made to be what I am—
anyone's lover. If you remove what God
has given me—my smile, my tender curls and
easy nakedness—your scrabbling hands, not
my fingers, will shrivel, dry as your man-

parts dried last night, again this morning. Man,
against your will I feel you swell and ease for
Yahweh who made you, like me, lower not
equal, with his airy angels. I am
your land: your hills, your shadowed valley and
your story. Tell me. You love your God

who loosens the rain when he will, your God
who shut the Red Sea's doors upon the men
of obedient Egyptian women and
their swaddled, unnamed babies for
amazement's sake. Why should your great I Am
blame you for loving me? I'm slurred, though not

as hard as He. Hear your prayer: *Cast me not
away from your presence, restore, O God,
the joy of your salvation.* If I am
your joy (I've heard you moan like other men),
uphold me now with your freed spirit, for
I tremble like a bird from Egypt and

a new child settles in me as ill-named and
well-fathered as my others. I cannot
help that I love infants, men or you; for
I have been made adulterous by God,
his own loose metaphor, confusing man
about the chords of love and freedom. I am

the doll you played with as a boy. I am
the one you put away—you loved me and
you feared that anyone would know. Poor man,
is there sufficient love for all? You'll not
sleep alone in the milk-filled land your God
has given everyone. Restore me, for

God, I am a woman and not a man.

Nola Garrett

The Greek Poets

Homer (8th Century B.C.?)

For Homer's Mosquito*

I read the song of Ilion,
Of men who fought and died
While sunlight lingered, shining on
This and the other side.

I read the names of famous men
Who lifted heavy spears
And shields they would not use again.
I listened down the years:

Distinct above the battle ground,
Insistent through the din,
A whining hum, a singing sound,
Mosquito diving in.

As brave as that, blind Homer said,
Who knew the tones of fear:
Thirsty for blood, to danger bred,
Mosquito feeding here.

So Homer sings: so Hector dies,
Achilles triumphs so.
High in the air an insect cries
The Ilion we know.

Ann Hayes

*See the *Iliad,* Book 17, lines 571-573 in Richard Lattimore's translation.

from *Calypso**

I

CALYPSO
*(perceiving the
long-wandering
Odysseus, clamber-
ing ashore)*

Clumsy futility, drown yourself—
did I ask you to this rock-shelf,
did I lure you here?
did I call, far and near,
come, come Odysseus,
you, you alone
are the unmatchable mate,
my own?
sea-nymph may sing;
I didn't say anything
even to the air;
I was alone,
bound hair,
unbound
and let it fall,
wound in no fillet or any pearl
nor coral,
only nodded
peaceful things;
I asked no wings
to lift me to mid-heaven,
to drop me to earth;
I was alone
now
my beautiful peace has gone;

did I ask you here?
O laugh, most intimate waters,
little cove
and the answering ripples
of the spring
that sends clear water to the salt,
tell me,

did I whisper to you ought
that would work a charm?
did I, unwittingly,
invoke some swallow
to fly low,
to beat into the hollow
of those great eyes,
stupid as an ox,
wide with surprise?
did I? did I?
I am priestess, occult, nymph and goddess,
then what was my fault?
there must have been fault somewhere,
in the wind,
in the air,
some counter-trick
to mock magic,
some counter-smile,
some malign goddess
to smile awry,

O see, Calypso, poor girl,
is caught at last;

O oaf, O ass,
O any slow, plodding and silly animal,
O man,
I am amused to think you may fall;
here where I feel
maiden hair,
where I clutch the root of the sea-bay,
where I slide a thin foot along
a crack,
you will slip;
you are heavy,
great oaf,
walrus,
whale, clumsy on land,

clumsy with your great arms with an oar
at sea;
you have no wit in the air,
you are fit only to clamber
to climb, then to fall;
then to fall;
you will slide clumsy
unto the sand

. . . . .

Idiot;
did he think he could reach the ledge?
why, already he leans over the edge;
he is dizzy,
he will fall—
shout, shout O sea-gulls,
large pickings for the wrasse, the eel;
we eat Odysseus, the land-walrus,
to-morrow with parsley
and bean-sauce—
eat,
that's what I could do;
eat fruit—
drink deep from crystal bowl—

. . . . .

II

CALYPSO   O you clouds,
(on land)   here is my song;
                     man is clumsy and evil,
                     a devil.

                     O you sand,
                     here is my command,
                     drown all men in slow breathless suffocation—
                     then they may understand.

O you winds,
beat his sails flat,
shift a wave sideways
that he suffocate.

O you waves,
run counter to his oars,
waft him to blistering shores,
where he may die of thirst.

O you skies,
send rain
to wash salt from my eyes,

and witness all earth and heaven,
it was of my heart-blood
his sails were woven;

witness, river and sea and land;
you, you must hear me—
man is a devil,
man will not understand.

ODYSSEUS
(on the sea)

She gave me fresh water in an earth-jar,
strange fruits
to quench thirst,
a golden zither
to work magic on the water;

she gave me wine in a cup
and white wine in a crystal shell;
she gave me water and salt,
wrapped in a palm leaf
and palm-dates

she gave me wool and a pelt of fur,
she gave me a pelt of silver-fox,
and a brown soft skin of a bear,

she gave me an ivory comb for my hair,
she washed brine and mud from my body,
and cool hands
held balm
for a rust-wound;

she gave me water
and fruit in a basket,
and shallow
baskets of pulse and grain, and a ball
of hemp
for mending the sail;

she gave me a willow basket
for letting into the shallows
for eels;

she gave me peace in her cave.

CALYPSO
(from land)

He has gone,
he has forgotten;
he took my lute and my shell of crystal—
he never looked back—

ODYSSEUS
(on the sea)

She gave me a wooden flute,
and a mantle
she wove of this wool—

CALYPSO
(from land)

—for man is a brute and a fool.

H.D.

---

*In the *Odyssey,* Calypso was a divine nymph who, for love of Odysseus, detained him on her island for seven years, offering immortality if he would remain with her. Odysseus continued to pine for home and family until finally, at the gods' request, Calypso released him and helped him to return.

from *Circe / Mud Poems**

✻

I made no choice
I decided nothing

One day you simply appeared in your stupid boat,
your killer's hands, your disjointed body, jagged as a shipwreck,
skinny-ribbed, blue-eyed, scorched, thirsty, the usual,
pretending to be—what? a survivor?

Those who say they want nothing
want everything.
It was not this greed
that offended me, it was the lies.

Nevertheless I gave you
the food you demanded for the journey
you said you planned; but you planned no journey
and we both knew it.

You've forgotten that,
you made the right decision.
The trees bend in the wind, you eat, you rest,
you think of nothing,
your mind, you say,
is like your hands, vacant:

vacant is not innocent.

✻

There must be more for you to do
than permit yourself to be shoved
by the wind from coast
to coast to coast, boot on the boat prow
to hold the wooden body
under, soul in control

Ask at my temples
where the moon snakes, tongues of the dark
speak like bones unlocking, leaves falling
of a future you won't believe in.

Ask who keeps the wind
Ask what is sacred

Don't you get tired of killing
those whose deaths have been predicted
and are therefore dead already?

Don't you get tired of wanting
to live forever?

Don't you get tired of saying Onward?

Margaret Atwood

*Circe, in the *Odyssey,* was a beautiful enchantress who changed men into swine. After his com-
panions met this fate, Odysseus, with help from the god Hermes, broke Circe's magic, which
caused her to fall in love with him. He remained with her for a year before continuing on his
way.

Siren Song*

This is the one song everyone
would like to learn: the song
that is irresistible:

the song that forces men
to leap overboard in squadrons
even though they see the beached skulls

the song nobody knows
because anyone who has heard it
is dead, and the others can't remember.

Shall I tell you the secret
and if I do, will you get me
out of this bird suit?

I don't enjoy it here
squatting on this island
looking picturesque and mythical

with these two feathery maniacs,
I don't enjoy singing
this trio, fatal and valuable.

I will tell the secret to you,
to you, only to you.
Come closer. This song

is a cry for help: Help me!
Only you, only you can,
you are unique

at last. Alas
it is a boring song
but it works every time.

Margaret Atwood

*The Sirens, in the *Odyssey,* were sea creatures, half bird and half woman, whose irresistible singing lured sailors to their deaths.

The Wife of the Man of Many Wiles*

Believe what you want to. Believe that I wove,
If you wish, twenty years, and waited, while you
were knee-deep in blood, hip-deep in goddesses.

I've not much to show for twenty years' weaving—
I have but one half-finished cloth at the loom.
Perhaps it's the lengthy, meticulous grieving.

Explain how you want to. Believe I unravelled
At night what I stitched in the slow siesta,
How I kept them all waiting for me to finish,

The suitors, you call them. Believe what you want to.
Believe that they waited for me to finish,
Believe I beguiled them with nightly undoings.

Believe what you want to. That they never touched me.
Believe your own stories, as you would have me do,
How you only survived by the wise infidelities.

Believe that each day you wrote me a letter
That never arrived. Kill all the damn suitors
If you think it will make you feel better.

A.E. Stallings

*Penelope, wife of Odysseus, waited twenty years for him to return from the Trojan War.
Courted by more than a hundred suitors, she promised to remarry once she had finished weav-
ing a shroud for Odysseus' father. Each night she unravelled her day's work, and thus kept her
suitors at bay. For yet another revision of Penelope's story, see (in this volume) "Penelope and
Ulysses Settle a Domestic Dispute," a response by Joyce La Mers to Tennyson's "Ulysses."

Alcaeus (7th–6th Century B.C.)

To Alcaeus

> who said to Sappho, "I fain would speak
> to you, but shame restrains me."

Were your desiring good and fair
And did your tongue no ill prepare,
Then had no shame possessed your sight
But you had pled your plea outright.

Sappho
translated by J.M. Edmonds

Anacreon (c. 570–? B.C.)

Anachronism*

(for Anacreon)

Married.
Drank red wine.
Broke the glasses.

Had children
like pumpkins on a vine
waiting for Halloween
to see their faces.

Loved all
forbidden fruit—
steak, chocolate cake,
whipped cream, sex for fun,
red wine.

Listened
to Mozart, Dvorak,
Beethoven, Shostakovitch.
Drank red wine.

Remember when
the ocean was clean,
comics were funny,
only Camels were smoked.

Remember worrying
about getting knocked up,
not getting a husband,
getting fat, getting drunk, not AIDS.

Learned "Fern Hill" by silly heart.
Fell in love with life
and half in love
with easeful death.

Now.
Drink red wine when I can
with dying friends.

Drink brandy alone
at bedtime
learning "Sailing to Byzantium"
by cussed heart.

B.B. Adams

*Anacreon was so popular with the ancient Greeks, primarily for his drinking songs and poems of playful, erotic love, that a statue of him was placed on the Acropolis.

Sophocles (496–406/5 B.C.)

The Daughters of Oedipus*

Antigone, Choosing Her Death

He will argue since I was so good
at digging (see? the dirt still grouts my nails),
that while my breath held out I could have clawed
the rock away. Impossible. This jail's
plainly a tomb where I am meant to beat
the walls until I crumble. While the scent
of life survives, I claim the right to cheat
him of the sight he craves: these fingers, spent,
my face grown stiff and old with panic. Pride
impelled us both toward mastery: He'd have
me battle suffocation just as I'd
fought the ban against my brother's grave;
but if I lift my head and knot the cord—
like this—then, Creon, which of us is lord?

Ismene, Remembering Her Sister

I am ordinary. Greatness never
even winked at me but once. Unready
for the risk, I forfeited forever
any chance for glory. Being steady,
politic, I withheld what love
demanded—while Antigone embraced
disaster like a faithful daughter of
the house of Labdacus, born to taste
the Furies' vengeance with the rest: that mother
acting the unspeakable, our blind
father groping for atonement, brother

killing brother. I alone can find
no destiny. My life is drawn so small
the gods have no design for me at all.

Grace Simpson

*In the Sophocles play bearing her name, Antigone buries the body of her brother Polyneices, defying the orders of her uncle, King Creon. Creon sentences Antigone to be entombed alive, but she commits suicide in the cave where she has been placed. Ismene, timid and acquiescent, has a minor role in the family drama and disappears without explanation at the end of the play.

Euripides (485–406 B.C.)

Medea, Homesick*

How many gifted witches, young and fair,
Have flunked, been ordinary, left the back-
Stooping study of their art, black
Or white, for love, that sudden foreigner?
Because chalk-fingered Wisdom streaks the hair,
Because the flame that flaps upon its wick
Rubrics the eye, I left behind the book
And washed my hands of ink, my homeland, my father.
But beauty doesn't travel well: the ocean,
Sun-strong years. The charms I knew by rote,
Irregular as verbs, decline to charm.
I cannot spell the simplest old potion
I learned for love. As for the antidote,
He discovered it himself, and is past harm.

A.E. Stallings

*Medea was a sorceress who, for love of Jason, used her magical arts to help him steal the Golden Fleece from her father. Euripides' play takes up the story after the couple had fled to Corinth. When Jason abandoned Medea for the daughter of King Creon, Medea took revenge by murdering the king, his daughter, and her own two children by Jason.

Medea's Soliloquy

Why didn't I just carry off
his second wife and win her over?
That's a revenge to make enough
impression on a faithless lover.

We could be back in Colchis now.
I have no doubt she'd have been willing
to overthrow the selfish hound...
anyway, I'd have saved the killing

of my two boys...that part was hard
even for me, a lovely hater.
But anger carries a sharp sword—
the better thought came one day later.

                                        Gail White

Plato (c.428–c.348 B.C.)

Lais*

Let her who walks in Paphos
take the glass,
let Paphos take the mirror
and the work of frosted fruit,
gold apples set
with silver apple-leaf,
white leaf of silver
wrought with veins of gilt.

Let Paphos lift the mirror,
let her look
into the polished centre of the disk.

Let Paphos take the mirror,
did she press
flowerlet of flame-flower
to the lustrous white
of the white forehead?
did the dark veins beat
a deeper purple
than the wine-deep tint
of the dark flower?

Did she deck black hair
one evening, with the winter-white
flower of the winter-berry,
did she look (reft of her lover)
at a face gone white
under the chaplet
of white virgin-breath?
Lais, exultant, tyrannizing Greece,

Lais who kept her lovers in the porch,
lover on lover waiting,
(but to creep
where the robe brushed the threshold
where still sleeps Lais)
so she creeps, Lais,
to lay her mirror at the feet
of her who reigns in Paphos.

Lais has left her mirror
for she sees no longer in its depth
the Lais' self
that laughed exultant
tyrannizing Greece.

Lais has left her mirror,
for she weeps no longer,
finding in its depth,
a face, but other
than dark flame and white
feature of perfect marble.

Lais has left her mirror,
(so one wrote)
to her who reigns in Paphos;
Lais who laughed a tyrant over Greece,
Lais who turned the lovers from the porch,
that swarm for whom now
Lais has no use;
Lais is now no lover of the glass,
seeing no more the face as once it was,
wishing to see that face and finding this.

H.D.

*Author's note: "The poem Lais has in italics a translation of the Plato epigram in the *Greek Anthology*."

Meleager (c. 100 b.c.)

*Heliodora**

He and I sought together,
over the spattered table,
rhymes and flowers,
gifts for a name.

He said, among others, I will bring
(and the phrase was just and good,
but not as good as mine,)
"the narcissus that loves the rain."

We strove for a name,
while the light of lamps burnt thin
and the outer dawn came in,
a ghost, the last at the feast
or the first,
to sit within
with the two that remained
to quibble in flowers and verse
over a girl's name.

He said, "the rain, loving,"
I said, "the narcissus, drunk,
drunk with the rain."

Yet I had lost
for he said,
"the rose, the lover's gift,
is loved of love,"
he said it,
"loved of love;"
I waited, even as he spoke,

to see the room filled with a light,
as when in winter
the embers catch in a wind
when a room is dank;
so it would be filled, I thought,
our room with a light
when he said
(and he said it first,)
"the rose, the lover's delight,
is loved of love,"
but the light was the same.

Then he caught,
seeing the fire in my eyes,
my fire, my fever, perhaps,
for he leaned
with the purple wine
stained on his sleeve,
and said this:
"did you ever think
a girl's mouth
caught in a kiss,
is a lily that laughs?"

I had not.
I saw it now
as men must see it forever afterwards;
no poet could write again,
"the red-lily,
a girl's laugh caught in a kiss;"
it was his to pour in the vat
from which all poets dip and quaff,
for poets are brothers in this.

So I saw the fire in his eyes,
it was almost my fire,
(he was younger,)
I saw the face so white,

my heart beat,
it was almost my phrase;
I said, "surprise the muses,
take them by surprise;
it is late,
rather it is dawn-rise;
those ladies sleep, the nine,
our own king's mistresses."

A name to rhyme,
flowers to bring to a name,
what was one girl faint and shy,
with eyes like the myrtle,
(I said: "her underlids
are rather like the myrtle,")
to vie with the nine?

Let him take the name,
he had the rhymes,
"the rose, loved of love,
the lily, a mouth that laughs,"
he had the gift,
"the scented crocus,
the purple hyacinth,"
what was one girl to the nine?

He said:
"I will make her a wreath;"
he said:
"I will write it thus:

I will bring you the lily that laughs,
I will twine
with soft narcissus, the myrtle,
sweet crocus, white violet,
the purple hyacinth, and last,
the rose, loved-of-love,
that these may drip on your hair

the less soft flowers,
may mingle sweet with the sweet
of Heliodora's locks,
myrrh-curled."
(He wrote myrrh-curled,
I think, the first.)

I said:
"they sleep, the nine,"
when he shouted swift and passionate:
"*that* for the nine!
above the hills
the sun is about to wake,
and to-day white violets
shine beside white lilies
adrift on the mountain side;
to-day the narcissus opens
that loves the rain."

I watched him to the door,
catching his robe
as the wine-bowl crashed to the floor,
spilling a few wet lees,
(ah, his purple hyacinth!)
I saw him out the door,
I thought:
there will never be a poet
in all the centuries after this,
who will dare write,
after my friend's verse,
"a girl's mouth
is a lily kissed."

                                                              H.D.

*Author's note: "Heliodora has in italics the two Meleager epigrams from the *Greek Anthology*."

Nossis*

I thought to hear him speak
the girl might rise
and make the garden silver,
as the white moon breaks,
"Nossis," he cried, "a flame."

I said:
"a girl that's dead
some hundred years;
a poet—what of that?
for in the islands,
in the haunts of Greek Ionia,
Rhodes and Cyprus,
girls are cheap."

I said, to test his mood,
to make him rage or laugh or sing or weep,
"in Greek Ionia and in Cyprus,
many girls are found
with wreaths and apple-branches."

"Only a hundred years or two or three,
has she lain dead
yet men forget;"
he said,
"I want a garden,"
and I thought
he wished to make a terrace on the hill,
bend the stream to it,
set out daffodils,
plant Phrygian violets,
such was his will and whim,
I thought,
to name and watch each flower.

His was no garden
bright with Phrygian violets,
his was a shelter
wrought of flame and spirit,
and as he flung her name
against the dark,
I thought the iris-flowers
that lined the path
must be the ghosts of Nossis.

"Who made the wreath,
for what man was it wrought?
speak, fashioned all of fruit-buds,
song, my loveliest,
say Meleager brought to Diocles,
(a gift for that enchanting friend)
memories with names of poets.
He sought
for Moero, lilies,
and those many,
red-lilies for Anyte,
for Sappho, roses,

with those few, he caught
that breath of the sweet-scented
leaf of iris,
the myrrh-iris,
to set beside the tablet
and the wax
which love had burnt,
when scarred across by Nossis:"

when she wrote:

"I Nossis stand by this:
I state that love is sweet:
if you think otherwise
assert what beauty

or what charm
after the charm of love,
retains its grace?
"Honey," you say:
honey? I say "I spit
honey out of my mouth:
nothing is second-best
after the sweet of Eros."

I Nossis stand and state
that he whom Love neglects
has naught, no flower, no grace,
who lacks that rose, her kiss."

I thought to hear him speak
the girl might rise
and make the garden silver
as the white moon breaks,
"Nossis," he cried, "a flame."

H.D.

*Author's note: "In Nossis is the translation of the opening lines of the Garland of Meleager and the poem of Nossis herself in the *Greek Anthology*."

The Latin Poets

Catullus (c. 84–c. 54 B.C.)

To Catullus—Highet

(A response to the Highet translation of Catullus 70)

My lover says he'd want to lie with none
but me, even if Venus herself welcomed his wooing.
Oh yes! but what a man will say to an older woman,
    write it on thin air, read on the run.

Kelly Cherry

From a Letter from Lesbia*

...So, praise the gods, Catullus is away!
    And let me tend you this advice, my dear:
Take any lover that you will or may
    Except a poet. All of them are queer.

It's just the same—a quarrel or a kiss
    Is but a tune to play upon his pipe.
He's always hymning that or wailing this;
    Myself, I much prefer the business type.

That thing he wrote, the time the sparrow died—
    (Oh, most unpleasant—gloomy, tedious words!)
I called it sweet, and made believe I cried;
    The stupid fool! I've always hated birds....

Dorothy Parker

*"That thing he wrote": see Catullus III.

Virgil (70—19 B.C.)

Dido of Tunisia*

I had heard of these things before—of chariots rumbling
      Through the desolate streets, of the battle cries and the danger,
And the flames rising up, and the walls of the houses crumbling.
      It was told to me by a stranger.

But it was for love of the fair and long-robed Helen,
      The stranger said (his name still troubles my sleep),
That they came to the windy town he used to dwell in,
      Over the wine-dark deep.

In the hollow ships they came, though the cost was dear.
      And the towers toppled, the heroes were slain without pity.
But whose white arms have beckoned these armies here
      To trample my wasted city?

Ah, this, Aeneas, you did not tell me of:
That men might struggle and fall, and not for love.

Phyllis McGinley

*In Virgil's *Aeneid,* Aeneas was shipwrecked while sailing from Troy and received by Dido, Queen of Carthage. She fell in love with him and committed suicide after he left her.

Eurydice Reveals Her Strength*

Dying is the easy part.
As you still live, my dear, why did you come?
You should learn an easing of the heart
As I have, now, for truly some

Prefer this clarity of mind, this death
Of all the body's imperious demands:
That constant interruption of the breath,
That fever-greed of eyes and hands

To digest your beauty whole.
You strike a tune upon a string:
They say that it is beautiful.
You sing to me, you sing, you sing.

I think, how do the living hear?
But I remember now, that it was just
A quiver in the membrane of the ear,
And love, a complicated lust.

And I remember now, as in a book,
How you pushed me down upon the grass and stones,
Crushed me with your kisses and your hands and took
What there is to give of emptiness, and moans.

We strained to be one strange new beast enmeshed,
And this is what we strained against, this death,
And clawed as if to peel away the flesh,
Crawled safe inside another's hollowness,

Because we feared this calm of being dead.
I say this. You abhor my logic, and you shiver,
Thinking I may as well be just some severed head
Floating down a cool, forgetful river,

Slipping down the shadows, green and black,
Singing to myself, not looking back.

A.E. Stallings

*In Virgil's *Georgics IV,* Eurydice was the wife of Orpheus, a master singer and player of the lyre.
When she was killed by a snake, he journeyed to the Underworld to plead for her release.
Hades agreed, on the condition that Orpheus did not look at her until they had completed their
ascent to upper Earth. Upon emerging into the light, Orpheus could not resist glancing back at
Eurydice, and she was plunged back into the Underworld.

Horace (65–8 B.C.)

*After Horace: The Pastor's Wife Delivers Soup**

Don't ask, Patricia Stone, when you will join
your husband, Horace, scattered in your garden.
Your hosta lilies thrive in shade beneath
his unpruned apple tree; your fountain drowns
the haste of Wesleyville. Here—eat this soup
and drink this milk—your bones are getting thin.
Why? Well—so are mine. I've got to run
arrange myself—the pastor's coming home.

Nola Garrett

*See Horace's "Carpe Diem Ode," Book I, #11.

Ovid (43 B.C.–17 A.D.)

Daphne*

Poet, Singer, Necromancer—
I cease to run. I halt you here,
Pursuer, with an answer.

Do what you will.
What blood you've set to music I
Can change to chlorophyll,

And root myself, and with my toes
Wind to subterranean streams.
Through solid rock my strength now grows.

Such now am I, I cease to eat,
But feed on flashes from your eyes;
Light, to my new cells, is meat.

Find then, when you seize my arm
That xylem thickens in my skin
And there are splinters in my charm.

I may give in; I do not lose.
Your hot stare cannot stop my shivering,
With delight, if I so choose.

A.E. Stallings

*Daphne, a virgin huntress fleeing an amorous Apollo, begged the gods for assistance and was turned into a laurel tree. This poem and the following three refer to Ovid's *Metamorphoses*.

Arachne Gives Thanks to Athena*

It is no punishment. They are mistaken—
The brothers, the father. My prayers were answered.
I was all fingertips. Nothing was perfect:
What I have woven, the moths will have eaten;
At the end of my rope was a noose's knot.

Now it's no longer the thing, but the pattern,
And that will endure, even though webs be broken.

I, if not beautiful, am beauty's maker.
Old age cannot rob me, nor cowardly lovers.
The moon once pulled blood from me. Now I pull silver.
Here are the lines I pulled from my own belly—
Hang them with rainbows, ice, dewdrops, darkness.

A.E. Stallings

*Arachne, a peasant girl, boasted that her weaving was the equal of Athena's, whereupon the goddess challenged her to a contest. Goddess and mortal finished their work at the same time, and it was indeed of equal beauty. Enraged, Athena changed Arachne into a spider. See also (in this volume) Toni La Ree Bennett's "Mezza Ragna," a response to Dante's portrayal of Arachne in his *Purgatorio.*

A Likely Story*

Atalanta, all her life,
Ran away from being wife.
How did she come in second place
In such a sprint? It was a race
She always used to win. To wit,
The blackguard tricked her into it,
But then, in love, it is no feat
To find a fellow who will cheat.

A.E. Stallings

*Atalanta, who could outrun any man, declared she would marry no one who could not first beat her in a foot race. After many suitors had tried and failed, Hippomenes enlisted the aid of Aphrodite, who gave him three golden apples so beautiful that no mortal could resist them. Hippomenes carried the apples to the race and threw them one by one across Atalanta's path. She stopped to gather them, he won the race, and they were married.

from *Philomela**

I.

In the night a winged man comes to me.
His feathered arms crush me, push me to the ground.
What I know is hidden by his body,

there is nothing but the endless tear,
the push and pull of unyielding flesh,
what he says is truth—this is what I've always wanted,
there is betrayal in my voice.

When he is spent, blame roots in me like his seed,
his talons slice the tongue from my mouth,
throw it to a flock of hungry, black-eyed birds.

He says I want him.

I do not struggle,
but imagine the rocking of my sister's arms
in the violent rhythm that has brought me here.
Then he is gone.

I bury what remains of my tongue
so the birds cannot feed on it,
use it to give voice to their song
while I am held by silence.

I have been here a long time.

II.

I am twelve years old
I wear my mother's clothes
Pretending they fit me
Though slightly loose

I wear my mother's clothes
Her white knit dress
Though slightly loose
Barely touches my breasts

In her white knit dress
I move with her rhythm
Barely touch my breasts
Shift hips and arms

Moving with her rhythm
I lift my shoulders
Shift hips and arms
The dress falls to the floor

I lift my shoulders
Released from my body

The dress falls to the floor
I trace circles between my thighs

Released from my body
I have become her
Tracing circles between my thighs
Crying for what she does not give

I have become her
Lover, her daughter, herself
Crying for what she does not give
The only thing I want

Lover, daughter, self
Boundaries blurred
The only thing I want
I give to her

Boundaries blurred
I cannot tell what
I give to her
What she has taken

I cannot tell you
My name
What she has taken
What I have left

My name
Worn by silence
What I have left
I can no longer wear

Worn in silence
What I pretend fits me
I can no longer wear
I am twelve years old.

III.

My sister,
we have eaten far too much,
scraped pain from the bones of our sons,
forged anger from our daughters' blood.

It is not time for sorrow.
It is the time to throw into the fire
what we've worn to mask our fury,
paint our faces ember red
and howl.

Beth Fein

*Philomela was the beautiful younger sister of Queen Procne, who was married to Tereus, King of Thrace and a son of Apollo. Tereus forced Philomela into a pretend marriage and, when she threatened to reveal his actions, cut out her tongue, abandoned her, and told the queen Philomela was dead. Philomela wove her story into a tapestry, had it sent to Procne, and the two sisters took revenge on Tereus. Procne was later turned into a nightingale, Philomela into a swallow. However, in Roman versions of the legend, and subsequently in the English poetic tradition, it is Philomela who is associated with the nightingale.

Juvenal (55?–138? A.D.)

*Pro Femina**

One

From Sappho to myself, consider the fate of women.
How unwomanly to discuss it! Like a noose or an albatross necktie
The clinical sobriquet hangs us: cod-piece coveters.
Never mind these epithets; I myself have collected some honeys.
Juvenal set us apart in denouncing our vices
Which had grown, in part, from having been set apart:
Women abused their spouses, cuckolded them, even plotted
To poison them. Sensing, behind the violence of his manner—
"Think I'm crazy or drunk?"—his emotional stake in us,
As we forgive Strindberg and Nietzsche, we forgive all those
Who cannot forget us. We *are* hyenas. Yes, we admit it.

While men have politely debated free will, we have howled for it,
Howl still, pacing the centuries, tragedy heroines.
Some who sat quietly in the corner with their embroidery
Were Defarges, stabbing the wool with the names of their ancient
Oppressors, who ruled by the divine right of the male—
I'm impatient of interruptions! I'm aware there were millions
Of mutes for every Saint Joan or sainted Jane Austen,
Who, vague-eyed and acquiescent, worshipped God as a man.
I'm not concerned with those cabbageheads, not truly feminine
But neutered by labor. I mean real women, like *you* and like *me.*

Freed in fact, not in custom, lifted from furrow and scullery,
Not obliged, now, to be the pot for the annual chicken,
Have we begun to arrive in time? With our well-known
Respect for life because it hurts so much to come out with it;
Disdainful of "sovereignty," "national honor," and other abstractions;
We can say, like the ancient Chinese to successive waves of invaders,

"Relax, and let us absorb you. You can learn temperance
In a more temperate climate." Give us just a few decades
Of grace, to encourage the fine art of acquiescence
And we might save the race. Meanwhile, observe our creative chaos,
Flux, efflorescence—whatever you care to call it!

Two

I take as my theme "The Independent Woman,"
Independent but maimed: observe the exigent neckties
Choking violet writers; the sad slacks of stipple-faced matrons;
Indigo intellectuals, crop-haired and callous-toed,
Cute spectacles, chewed cuticles, aced out by full-time beauties
In the race for a male. Retreating to drabness, bad manners
And sleeping with manuscripts. Forgive our transgressions
Of old gallantries as we hitch in chairs, light our own cigarettes,
Not expecting your care, having forfeited it by trying to get even.

But we need dependency, cosseting and well-treatment.
So do men sometimes. Why don't they admit it?
We will be cows for a while, because babies howl for us,
Be kittens or bitches, who want to eat grass now and then
For the sake of our health. But the role of pastoral heroine
Is not permanent, Jack. We want to get back to the meeting.

Knitting booties and brows, tartars or termagants, ancient
Fertility symbols, chained to our cycle, released
Only in part by devices of hygiene and personal daintiness,
Strapped into our girdles, held down, yet uplifted by man's
Ingenious constructions, holding coiffures in a breeze,
Hobbled and swathed in whimsey, tripping on feminine
Shoes with fool heels, losing our lipsticks, you, me,
In ephemeral stockings, clutching our handbags and packages.

Our masks, always in peril of smearing or cracking,
In need of continuous check in the mirror or silverware,
Keep us in thrall to ourselves, concerned with our surfaces.

Look at man's uniform drabness, his impersonal envelope!
Over chicken wrists or meek shoulders, a formal, hard-fibered assurance.
The drape of the male is designed to achieve self-forgetfulness.

So, Sister, forget yourself a few times and see where it gets you:
Up the creek, alone with your talent, sans everything else.
You can wait for the menopause, and catch up on your reading.
So primp, preen, prink, pluck and prize your flesh,
All posturings! All ravishment! All sensibility!
Meanwhile, have you used your mind today?
What pomegranate raised you from the dead,
Springing, full-grown, from your own head, Athena?

Three

I will speak about women of letters, for I'm in the racket.
Our biggest successes to date? Old maids to a woman.
And our saddest conspicuous failures? The married spinsters
On loan to husbands they treated like surrogate fathers.
Think of that crew of self-pitiers, not-very-distant,
Who carried the torch for themselves and got first-degree burns.
Or the sad sonneteers, toast-and-teasdales we loved at thirteen;
Middle-aged virgins seducing the puerile anthologists
Through lust-of the-mind; barbiturate-drenched Camilles
With continuous periods, murmuring softly on sofas
When poetry wasn't a craft but a sickly effluvium,
The air thick with incense, musk, and emotional blackmail.

I suppose they reacted from an earlier womanly modesty
When too many girls were scabs to their stricken sisterhood,
Impugning our sex to stay in good with the men,
Commencing their insecure bluster. How they must have swaggered
When women themselves endorsed their own inferiority!
Vestals, vassals and vessels, rolled into several,
They took notes in rolling syllabics, in careful journals,
Aiming to please a posterity that despises them.
But we'll always have traitors who swear that a woman surrenders

Her Supreme Function, by equating Art with aggression
And failure with Femininity. Still, it's just as unfair
To equate Art with Femininity, like a prettily packaged commodity
When we are the custodians of the world's best-kept secret:
Merely the private lives of one-half of humanity.

But even with masculine dominance, we mares and mistresses
Produced some sleek saboteuses, making their cracks
Which the porridge-brained males of the day were too thick to perceive,
Mistaking young hornets for perfectly harmless bumblebees.
Being thought innocuous rouses some women to frenzy;
They try to be ugly by aping the ways of the men
And succeed. Swearing, sucking cigars and scorching the bedspread,

Slopping straight shots, eyes blotted, vanity-blown
In the expectation of glory: *she writes like a man!*
This drives other women mad in a mist of chiffon.
(One poetess draped her gauze over red flannels, a practical feminist.)

But we're emerging from all that, more or less,
Except for some lady-like laggards and Quarterly priestesses
Who flog men for fun, and kick women to maim competition.
Now, if we struggle abnormally, we may almost seem normal;
If we submerge our self-pity in disciplined industry;
If we stand up and be hated, and swear not to sleep with editors;
If we regard ourselves formally, respecting our true limitations
Without making an unseemly show of trying to unfreeze our assets;
Keeping our heads and our pride while remaining unmarried;
And if wedded, kill guilt in its tracks when we stack up the dishes
And defect to the typewriter. And if mothers, believe in the luck of our
     children,
Whom we forbid to devour us, whom we shall not devour,
And the luck of our husbands and lovers, who keep free women.

                                                    Carolyn Kizer

*See Juvenal's *Satire VI,* which enumerates for more than six hundred lines the follies and vices
of the female sex. The Roman poet's tone and meter are echoed in Kizer's poem.

Medieval and Renaissance Poets

Dante Alighieri (1265–1321)

*Beatrice**

Send out the singers—let the room be still;
They have not eased my pain nor brought me sleep,
Close out the sun, for I would have it dark
That I may feel how black the grave will be.
The sun is setting, for the light is red,
And you are outlined in a golden fire,
Like Ursula upon an altar-screen.
Come, leave the light and sit beside my bed,
For I have had enough of saints and prayers.
Strange broken thoughts are beating in my brain,
They come and vanish and again they come.
It is the fever driving out my soul,
And Death stands waiting by the arras there.

Ornella, I will speak, for soon my lips
Shall keep a silence till the end of time.
You have a mouth for loving—listen then:
Keep tryst with Love before Death comes to tryst;
For I, who die, could wish that I had lived
A little closer to the world of men,
Not watching always through the blazoned panes
That show the world in chilly greens and blues
And grudge the sunshine that would enter in.
I was no part of all the troubled crowd
That moved beneath the palace windows here,
And yet sometimes a knight in shining steel
Would pass and catch the gleaming of my hair,
And wave a mailèd hand and smile at me.
I made no sign to him and turned away,
Frightened and yet glad and full of dreams.
Ah, dreams and dreams that asked no answering!

I should have wrought to make my dreams come true.
But all my life was like an autumn day,
Full of gray quiet and a hazy peace.

What was I saying? All is gone again.
It seemed but now I was the little child
Who played within a garden long ago.
Beyond the walls the festal trumpets blared.
Perhaps they carried some Madonna by
With tossing ensigns in a sea of flowers,
A painted Virgin with a painted Child,
Who saw for once the sweetness of the sun
Before they shut her in the altar-niche
Where tapers smoke against the windy gloom.
I gathered roses redder than my gown
And played that I was Saint Elizabeth,
Whose wine had turned to roses in her hands.
And as I played, a child came through the gate,
A boy who looked at me without a word,
As though he saw stretch far behind my head,
Long lines of radiant angels, row on row.
That day we spoke a little, timidly,
And after that I never heard his voice;
Never again in after years his voice
That sang so many songs for love of me.
He was content to stand and watch me pass,
To seek for me at matins every day,
Where I could feel his eyes, although I prayed.
I think if he had stretched his hands to me,
Or moved his lips to say a single word,
I might have loved him....

Ornella, are you there? I cannot see—
Is every one so lonely when he dies?

The room is filled with lights—with waving lights—
Who are the men and women round the bed?
What have I said, Ornella? Have they heard?

There was no evil hidden in my life,
And yet, oh never, never let them know—

Am I not floating in a mist of light?
Oh, lift me up and I shall reach the sun!

Sara Teasdale

*Beatrice, the Muse of Dante's poetry and his symbol of ideal womanhood through most of his life, was in real life Beatrice Portinari, daughter of a Florentine nobleman. Dante's obsession with Beatrice was based on few actual meetings (the first when both were nine years old, the second nine years later). She married another man and died at age twenty-four.

Mezza Ragna*

Purgatorio, Canto 12
O mad Arachne, I saw you already / half spider, wretched
on the ragged remnants / of work that you had wrought
to your own hurt! (vss. 43–45)

Stuck somewhere in the middle
mezza ragna, mezza donna
what sin is hers?

She was the best, after all.
The sin, it might seem,
was to know it and
to show it, boasting, apparently,
being the sole prerogative
of a goddess.

But her real crime was to
ignore her teachers, the
ones who came before,
the wise women and goddesses
who taught her her art.

Like young women in a
"post-feminist" era who ask
what all the fuss is about,
Arachne considered
herself aboriginal, sprung
from a seed planted by no one.

Suspended from her web,
still permitted by divine pity
to practice her art,
Spider Woman must think,
somewhere between strands,
of how the goddess and the girl
are not that far apart
if the links between them
are not unnaturally severed.

She hangs still on a slim thread
between two possibilities—
mezza donna, mezza dea.

Toni La Ree Bennett

Mezza ragna: half spider; *mezza donna:* half woman; *mezza dea:* half goddess. For another view of
Arachne, see (in this volume) "Arachne Gives Thanks to Athena" by A.E. Stallings, in response
to Ovid's *Metamorphoses.*

No Pastel Princess

Purgatorio, Cantos 28–33

You expected maybe a
pastel princess from Oz?

You think you still feed
through the cord

from your mother's gut
and that you'll starve
if it's ever cut.

Put your tongue back
in your mouth, pilgrim.
This mama's not giving
up any milk today.

So take your wilted lilies
back to the florist;
she's not having any.

She may glow whenever
you come around, but
believe me, she's no Tinkerbelle,
although she's saved your butt
on more than one occasion.

Weren't you ever warned,
the more beautiful she gets,
the more her beauty hurts?

Haven't you learned by now
the only good Beatrice
is a dead Beatrice?

Little orphan Alighieri,
it's time to be your
own mother now
and put your playthings down.

Toni La Ree Bennett

Geoffrey Chaucer (c. 1340–1400)

After Many Years, Griselda Loses Patience*

> Ne suffreth nat that men yow doon offense.
> —Chaucer, "The Clerk's Tale" (1197)

Tonight, I saw him watching her again,
our daughter smiling at him as she poured his wine,
and I knew that time had at last wound out its skein:
there is nothing left to give him
but what he has already taken.

Love was never enough. It always fell short
of that thing he names *obedience*. I might call it
something else, something like death,
and fashion my face into a mask.
Tonight, while he sleeps, I'll take the iron from the fire,
I'll strike one blow for each tear swallowed unshed;
one for my tongue, bitten through and bloodied
as I held back from pleading; a blow for each of the children
taken from me and returned damaged, no longer mine;
a blow for every prayer ignored by unmerciful Heaven.

Tomorrow, they will not recognize
what I've made of him.

Kel Munger

*Griselda, in "The Clerk's Tale," is portrayed as the epitome of the patient, obedient, and long-suffering wife.

Sir Thomas Wyatt (1503–1542)

Whoso List to Hunt*

I will not live for you and so I die,
A pet too long domestic, though once wild.
The forest has grown strangely strange, and I,
Accustomed to your gardens, am grown mild.

For I, who once ate thorns and bitter bark,
Who out-stayed winter and who out-ran Death,
Stepped softly in the footsteps of the dark,
Perceived pursuers by a wisp of breath,

Am now grown fat on apples and sweet grass—
My softened senses dulled as if with age.
And while through savage freedoms now I pass,
Sometimes recall your arms, that gentle cage,

As wolves, who gather subtly, like lies,
Draw closer in, a noose of yellow eyes.

A.E. Stallings

*See Wyatt's poem of the same title.

William Shakespeare (1564–1616)

129 F. A Response to Shaxper's Sonnet 129

Th'expense of spirit as a def'nite act
Is pleasure shown; and showing, pleasure won
Distinctly, coming, going, nothing lacked,
Self-center'd, as tho' he the only one;
To sow, and so to spend, himself to sate:
With one concern; and afterward depressed,
With one concerned, content to lie and wait,
Then thought to lie in wait to him divest:
Divest of sacred jizzum, there's the rub;
Him, he, himself, the pleasure his to keep;
No bliss in her, noblesse oblige, no drug;
For her, to feel frustration; him, to sleep.
O, that this too, too stolid flesh would melt...
That rapture (all too often faked) be felt.

Dorothy Hickson

The Dark Lady Learns that Her Eyes Are Nothing Like the Sun*

Full many an amorous sonnet hast thou penned
    In praise of this one's hair and that one's eyes;
No scruples then—Nature was forced to bend
    Her simple truths to match thy fantasies.
Now sits St. Candour on thy spluttering quill;
    All grace, all compliment is now forgot,
And shall I answer that I love thee still,
    Or may the kettle vilify the pot?
Methinks this change of style appears too late;

Thy monarchy within my breast is done;
Lay in some other lap thy balding pate
  And close those eyes that could not bear the sun.
    At last the liberating truth be told:
    Or fact or false, all sonnets leave me cold.

Mary Holtby

*See Shakespeare's Sonnet 130.

Lady Macbeth on the Psych Ward

Doctor, I'm lost in these mazy halls that lead nowhere,
Sleepwalking through somebody else's nightmare
On Six North, wiping my hands on my hair.

There's blood on my hands, blood in my hair,
Blood between my pale scissoring legs where
It pools in my underpants—the fancy pair

I bought for him to watch me wear and not wear.
There is blood everywhere
And I am lost in it. Doctor, I breathe blood, not air.

Kelly Cherry

Gertrude to Hamlet

Inside, the turned liver,
the shiny capsules,
the taffeta

bladders and envelopes.
Would you divide
the anatomical

destinies of a heart?
I have no business
that is not a functioning

mystery to you,
a blooming peony
and a purse of tears.

Dust, ash
or nothingness,
what tears

in bursting waves,
ill-tempered stresses.
Say what you please

I am
up to my hands
in a split creature.

Which makes my body my own.
I live in it; I gather
my own into it. Otherwise,

who would you be,
beginning to be?
You wander my throne like measles.

Lee Upton

John Donne (1572–1631)

The Dead Flea*

'Tis true I am not weakened by this death,
And you still stand with bulging eyes and pants
Beside my bed, where I so wish to rest.
I flick the bits of flesh and wipe the blood
On linen square, unsullied until now.
But this will be the only stain you see,
   For tiny bites do not a marriage make.
   Away, and let me lie alone, asleep.
   Go scratch your itching in some other place.

Karen Donnelly

*See Donne's "The Flea."

Ann Wishes She'd Taken a Little More Heed*

Though sweet to lie, my lovely lay,
indiff'rent to th'unruly sun,
guess what? Th'eleventh's on the way.
Yes, once again we've been undone.

Katherine McAlpine

*Donne's elopement with Ann More—an offense against both civil and canon law—resulted for him in a period of imprisonment and unemployment. However, the couple's love for one another seems never to have faltered. Ann died in the sixteenth year of their marriage, shortly after the birth of their eleventh child. "Unruly sun" is taken from Donne's "The Sun Rising."

To Donne Rhyming*

    Busy young fool, unruly Donne,
     Why do you thus
So early in the day make such a fuss?
Must your emotions organise the sun?
    Paltry romantic, time and tide
     Wait on no poet's fantasies:
  The sun *will* rise, and through the day abide,
   And you and I have other business.
Love has its proper season—so does rhyme.
(The afternoon might be a better time.)

Mary Holtby

*See Donne's "The Sun Rising."

The Seventeenth-
Century Poets

Robert Herrick (1591–1674)

Non Carpe Diem

Enter gently this good day
unfold the folds of velvet rose

but neither mourn nor rage
against its stoney thorn,

there too dawn delivers.
Let light fall, fill the space

between these thighs, where gods
have drunk and danced for years

without our help. Come, sweet sir,
day will not be seized.

Pat Falk

Corinna's Not Going A-Maying

(the lady addresses Mr. Herrick)

I like to sleep late on these fine spring mornings
Or lie in bed dreaming and half-awake.
And here's some fool babbling about Aurora
Under my window. O for heaven's sake!

I don't intend to deck myself with flowers
And walk about spangled with gems of dew.

The other girls can play at being milkmaids.
I'd feel a perfect fool. And wouldn't you?

But to your pastoral theme of sticky greenery
You bring in kisses as a counterpoint…
And talk of early morning assignations…
Aha! I think we're coming to the point.

Life is so short! you cry. But on this subject
Enough (enough, already) has been said.
Death's night is long, but last night isn't over.
Pack it in, Bob. I'm going back to bed.

Gail White

George Herbert (1593–1633)

Dialogue

My friend George Herbert has been chiding me,
wielding his blend of wit and humor. He
who could have summoned patience to abide
a sword piercing his side
nevertheless
rebukes my thanklessness.

"Give thanks? to whom? for what?" I bridle, knowing
there have been cries like mine forever, going
backward through all our days. I find him still
in that small room pure will
keeps clean of doubt,
sweeping the world's dust out.

"Why, Love, who is our Father," says my friend,
"whose word is our beginning and our end.
Such thanks are what we owe; Love's debt was paid
by covenant once made
there, on the cross.
Love found, all else is loss."

Oh, to believe him right! But wrestling with
the difference between history and myth,
our short view down the barrel and the long
perspective of his song,
"Help me to go,"
I beg, "past what I know:

If I, who have three sons, shoot two, will one
on whimsy's lucky side kiss the warm gun
that spared him? I have brothers everywhere

beyond both luck and prayer.
Now for their sake
teach me what sense to make

of such a random love, such fatherhood."
"Picture a grub who measures every good
by the half inch of soil he curls in. Now
picture, with man's eyes, how
acre by acre
Earth surrounds him. Maker

to creature of his making—grub or man
or angel—is so infinite a span!
Will the grub teach the farmer husbandry?
It is enough to be,
to tend this nest
and trust Love for the rest."

"For your song's sake—not what you sing to prove—
I will give thanks." The clock chimes, my hands move,
the book slips from my lap: alone, at night,
unanswered—but not quite,
who at sleep's edge
enjoy such privilege.

Rhina P. Espaillat

A Feminist Interlude (17th Century)

The Prologue*

I

To sing of wars, of captains, and of kings,
Of cities founded, commonwealths begun,
For my mean pen are too superior things;
Or how they all, or each their dates have run
Let poets and historians set these forth,
My obscure lines shall not so dim their worth.

II

But when my wond'ring eyes and envious heart
Great Bartas' sugared lines do but read o'er,
Fool do I grudge the Muses did not part
'Twixt him and me that overfluent store;
A Bartas can do what a Bartas will
But simple I according to my skill.

III

From schoolboy's tongue no rhet'ric we expect,
Nor yet a sweet consort from broken strings,
Nor perfect beauty where's a main defect:
My foolish, broken, blemished Muse so sings,
And this to mend, alas, no art is able,
'Cause nature made it so irreparable.

IV

Nor can I, like that fluent sweet tongued Greek,
Who lisped at first, in future times speak plain.
By art he gladly found what he did seek,
A full requital of his striving pain.
Art can do much, but this maxim's most sure:
A weak or wounded brain admits no cure.

V

I am obnoxious to each carping tongue
Who says my hand a needle better fits,
A poet's pen all scorn I should thus wrong,
For such despite they cast on female wits:
If what I do prove well, it won't advance,
They'll say it's stol'n, or else it was by chance.

VI

But sure the antique Greeks were far more mild
Else of our sex, why feigned they those nine
And poesy made Calliope's own child;
So 'mongst the rest they placed the arts divine:
But this weak knot they will full soon untie,
The Greeks did nought, but play the fools and lie.

VII

Let Greeks be Greeks, and women what they are
Men have precedency and still excel,
It is but vain unjustly to wage war;
Men can do best, and women know it well.
Preeminence in all and each is yours;
Yet grant some small acknowledgment of ours.

VIII

And oh ye high flown quills that soar the skies,
And ever with your prey still catch your praise,
If e'er you deign those lowly lines your eyes,
Give thyme or parsley wreath, I ask no bays;
This mean and unrefined ore of mine
Will make your glist'ring gold but more to shine.

Anne Bradstreet

*"Great Bartas," mentioned in Stanza II, was Guillaume de Salluste, seigneur du Bartas (1544–1590), well known during his time for *La Semaine,* a long, ungainly, didactic poem about the creation of the world. The poem, in English translation, proved more popular in England than it had been in France and influenced the work of Sidney, Spenser, and Milton, among others.

In Witness of Women Poets*

Rhapsodius does not imagine women write:
how can the silly notion not be laughed at,
as at the supposition that the Rhapsode's
work is not his own.

It might be so.
Has Sir Rhapsode never seen the like?
You sons of muses really think you are the only ones
whom artful Phoebus draws on and in.

Wrong. Pallas nurses for us nymphs a like
wisdom, art and intellect. If just now
we are not too rich in arts and gifts like you,
we are still your like, fine Phoebus folk, in every part.

(Then, we may well pass over
just how well free-flowing art becomes you.

From youth Apollo offers you
inducements to mount Parnassus' height.)

You will not wholly deny knowing
that God and Nature grant us equal opposites,
that poetry is often not for us,
our times disjointed.

We don't lack motherwit,
only opportunity.
When arts are showered onto us as well as you,
we will be more like equals.

Susanna E. Zeidler
translated from the German
by Ronnie Apter

*Translator's note: "In classical Grecian times a rhapsode was a professional reciter of Homer and at times an improvisational poet. In 17th-century Europe, 'rhapsode' came to mean 'poet'; Rhapsodius was a stock *nom de plume* for a poet. Note that the -us ending is masculine.

"Phoebus Apollo was the Greek god who patronized poetry. Pallas Athene, goddess of war and wisdom, was not known as a patroness of poetry, either by men or women."

John Milton (1608–1674)

Milton's Books Promiscuously Read

> …how can we more safely, and with less danger, scout into the region of sin and falsity than by reading all manner of tractates and hearing all manner of reason? And this is the benefit which may be had of books promiscuously read.—*Areopagitica*

On the Coming of Spring

During the season when the optic nerve
still carries images of ancient gods
and hormones are excreted in prose poems,
your lustful Faunus finds an oread
who flies on trembling feet but plays the game
called Hide-and-Seek or Hard-to-Get or Tease.
Like an acquaintance rapist, you declare
the non-existence of unwilling women.

Lycidas

If Lycidas could somehow rise again,
expel the Irish water from his lungs,
find his way back to literary London,
browse through a secondhand anthology,
come across the list of common flowers
tossed into the grave he shares with dolphins,
he'd marvel at the elegiac fuss
over an ordinary accident.

Samson Agonistes

What better option does Delilah have
than charming Samson with exotic dance,
turning him into an impotent skinhead?
Is she to be admonished or admired
for putting career before relationships?
And doesn't Samson choose his own afflictions
by sharing secrets in the afterglow
of intertribal, unprotected sex?

Paradise Lost

Not only do you blame the fall of man
on Satan, minimizing Eve's involvement,
but in your darkened eyes a woman's place
is where her husband puts her: nonconformist,
you make love to a trilogy of wives,
kill two with sperm-induced female afflictions,
spare only the third—Elizabeth—who serves
your memory by blabbering to Aubrey.

Areopagitica

When censors threaten freedom of the press,
would you support experimental art
that claims high purpose and intrinsic merit
but offers public acts of masturbation?
Or would you build a purifying pyre,
shut both damaged eyes while flames consume
everything that anyone finds offensive—
then feed your copy of the First Amendment?

Joanne Seltzer

Afterthought

> . . .O why did God,
> Creator wise, that peopled highest heaven
> With spirits masculine, create at last
> This novelty on earth, this fair defect
> Of nature, and not fill the world at once
> With men and angels without feminine?
> — *Paradise Lost*

Epimetheus, as an afterthought, blamed
his wife, Pandora, when he himself
forced open her box, dispersing all
her gifts. Did Adam likewise finger Eve
for giving life to his own earthy desires?

Imagine the first man in anaesthetic
slumber, antiseptic incision in his chest,
Adam's ethereal vision: a woman clothed
with the sun, under her feet the moon, gracing
her head a crown emblazoned with twelve stars.

Imagine his waking to Eve, a woman merely
human. Perhaps he believed the absent scar
a perverse reminder of something missing
—not in himself but a failing in her:
her refusal to embody his blessèd dream.

Imagine that Eve resisted the snake's advances,
obliging the devil to try the man. *Knowledge*
of good and evil, he'd brandish the fruit,
the power—to recreate Eve! Could Adam
have fallen for that old serpent's con?

After swallowing the intoxicating pap,
did Adam spot his former vision, strip her
of celestial light, and fabricate another
Eve arrayed in scarlet and purple, decked
with gold, precious stones and pearls?

Did Adam, high as a god, accost the real
woman, force open her lips to his will,
swelled with venom? And, after he came
down, noting his pillaged grace, did this man
soberly blame his victim for the rape?

Maxianne Berger

Milton's Women with Memories More than 300 Years Old

> . . .Oh! why did God,
> Creator wise, that peopled highest Heaven
> With Spirits masculine, create at last
> This novelty on Earth, this fair defect
> Of Nature?. . .

Milton had 3 wives, 3 daughters, blindness and poetry.
His only son died in infancy. Too bad he never
thought much of women: "irrational, liars, cheats
and seducers." He had needs. He couldn't write
every minute. He had to sleep, have someone to wash
his linen and cook and embrace. Did you think
we wouldn't remember and someday write of your
weakness for flesh, ragged breath and awkward
fumblings? Irrational, yes; but cunning, too,
and infinitely vengeful.

Laurel Speer

Richard Lovelace (1618–1658)

Lucasta Remains Unconvinced*

"Honour," you say, and think I'm unaware
of what you plan on chasing over there?

Katherine McAlpine

Lucasta Replies to Richard Lovelace*

Tell me not, Dick, I should be glad
  You're going to the wars;
Go if you must, I'll not be sad—
  But don't expect applause!

Women must ever wait and weep,
  They say, while men must fight—
There's more to do in bed than sleep
  Through every lonely night.

So don't think that I'll wait for you,
  Chaste as any nun;
You to honour will be true—
  I to having fun!

Margaret Rogers

*See "To Lucasta, Going to the Wars."

Andrew Marvell (1621–1678)

Coy Mistress

Sir, I am not a bird of prey:
a Lady does not seize the day.
I trust that brief Time will unfold
our youth, before he makes us old.
How could we two write lines of rhyme
were we not fond of numbered Time
and grateful to the vast and sweet
trials his days will make us meet?
The Grave's not just the body's curse;
no skeleton can pen a verse!
So while this numbered World we see,
let's sweeten Time with poetry,
and Time, in turn, may sweeten Love
and give us time our love to prove.
You've praised my eyes, forehead, breast:
you've all our lives to praise the rest.

Annie Finch

His Coy Mistress Replies

Andrew Marvell, you haven't read
Cosmo on women's wants in bed;
I loaned it you because you need
To learn there's more to love than speed.
You're like most men—a grope, a poke
Quick as you can, and then a smoke,
While women, Andrew, choose a pace

That's gentler than a half-mile race—
A slower, satisfying screw:
You've heard of foreplay, haven't you?

What transport schedules both of us—
Are you afraid you'll miss your bus?
My biological clock ticks true;
Your non-stop pleadings just won't do,
And lines about a private grave
Won't influence how I behave;
My "youthful hew" (how quaint your phrase!)
Will outlast all your reckless days.

And "tear our pleasures"?—dear, desist!
Are you a sadomasochist?
No, sweetheart, *slowly:* let's stretch time
And touch the stars with arts sublime,
Not squander all our precious leisure:
Our mutual purpose is: our pleasure.

D.A. Prince

The Eighteenth–
Century Poets

Jonathan Swift (1667–1745)

*Hypocrite Swift**

Hypocrite Swift now takes an eldest daughter.
He lifts Vanessa's hand. Cudsho, my dove!
Drink Wexford ale and quaff down Wexford water
But never love.

He buys new caps; he and Lord Stanley ban
Hedge-fellows who have neither wit nor swords.
He turns his coat; Tories are in; Queen Anne
Makes twelve new lords.

The town mows hay in hell; he swims in the river;
His giddiness returns; his head is hot.
Berries are clean, while peaches damn the giver
(Though grapes do not).

Mrs. Vanhomrigh keeps him safe from the weather.
Preferment pulls his periwig askew.
Pox takes belittlers; do the willows feather?
God keep you.

Stella spells ill; Lords Peterborough and Fountain
Talk politics; the Florence wine went sour.
Midnight: two different clocks, here and in Dublin,
Give out the hour.

On walls at court, long gilded mirrors gaze.
The parquet shines; outside the snow falls deep.
Venus, the Muses stare above the maze.
Now sleep.

Dream the mixed, fearsome dream. The satiric word
Dies in its horror. Wake, and live by stealth.

The bitter quatrain forms, is here, is heard,
Is wealth.

What care I; what cares saucy Presto? Stir
The bed-clothes; hearten up the perishing fire.
Hypocrite Swift sent Stella a green apron
And dead desire.

Louise Bogan

*"Vanessa" and "Stella," mentioned in many of Swift's poems, were his names for two much-younger women with whom he had intense (though probably unconsummated) relationships. Vanessa's real name was Esther Vanhomrigh; Stella, to whom he wrote several charming birthday poems, was Esther Johnson.

"If It Be True"*

If it be true, celestial Powers,
   That you have formed me fair,
And yet in all my vainest hours
   My mind has been my care;
Then in return I beg this grace,
   As you were ever kind:
What envious Time takes from my face,
   Bestow upon my mind.

Esther Johnson

*Esther Johnson often replied, in verse, to the poems Swift wrote for her birthday. It seems likely that the above, with its reference to the passing of time, was one of those replies.

The Gentleman's Study, In Answer to The Lady's Dressing-Room*

Some write of angels, some of goddess,
But I of dirty human bodies,
And lowly I employ my pen,
To write of naught but odious men;
And man I think, without a jest,
More nasty than the nastiest beast.

  In house of office, when they're bare,
And have not paper then to spare,
Their hands they'll take, half clean their bottom,
And daub the wall, O———rot 'em;
And in a minute, with a t——d,
They'll draw them out a beast or bird,
And write there without ink or pen:
When finger's dry, there's a——se again.
But now high time to tell my story;
But 'tis not one to all men's glory.

  A milliner, one Mrs. South,
I had the words from her own mouth,
That had a bill, which was long owing
By Strephon, for cloth, lace and sewing;
And on a day to's lodging goes,
In hopes of payment for the clothes,
And meeting there, and 'twas by chance,
His valet Tom, her old acquaintance,
Who, with an odd but friendly grin,
Told her his master's not within,
But bid her if she pleased to stay,
He'd treat her with a pot of tea;
So brought her to the study, while
He'd go and make the kettle boil.

  She sat her down upon the chair,
For that was all that then was there,

And turned her eyes on every side,
Where strange confusion she espied.

There on a block a wig was set,
Whose inside did so stink with sweat;
The outside oiled with jessamine,
T'disguise the stench that was within.

And next a shirt, with gussets red,
Which Strephon slept in, when in bed;
But modesty forbids the rest,
It shan't be spoke, but may be guessed;
A napkin worn upon a head,
Enough, infection to have bred.

For there some stocks lay on the ground,
One side was yellow, t'other brown;
And velvet breeches (on her word),
The inside all bedaubed with t——d,
And just before, I'll not desist
To let you know they were be-pissed:
Four different stinks lay there together,
Which were sweat, turd, and piss, and leather.

There in a heap lay nasty socks,
Here tangled stockings with silver clocks,
And towels stiff with soap and hair,
Of stinking shoes there lay a pair;
A nightgown, with gold rich-brocaded,
About the neck was sadly faded.

A close-stool helped to make the fume;
Tobacco-spits about the room,
With phlegm and vomit on the walls;
Here powder, dirt, combs and wash-balls;
Oil-bottles, paper, pens, and wax,
Dice, pamphlets, and of cards some packs;
Pig-tail and snuff, and dirty gloves,

Some plain, some fringed, which most he loves;
A curling-iron stands upright,
False locks and oil lay down close by't;
A drabbled cloak hung on a pin,
And basin furred with piss within;
Of pipes a heap, some whole, some broke,
Some cut-and-dry for him to smoke;
And papers that his a——se has cleaned,
And handkerchiefs with snuff all stained:
The sight and smells did make her sick,
She did not come to herself for a week.

  A coat that lay upon the table,
To reach so far she scarce was able,
But drew it to her resolved to try
What's in the pockets, by and by.

  The first thing that present her view
Were dunning-letters, not a few;
And then the next did make her wonder,
To see of tavern-bills such a number;
And a fine snuff-box lay there hid,
With bawdy picture in the lid,
And as she touched it, by the mass,
It turned, and showed a looking-glass.

  The rest she found, since I'm a-telling,
Advertisements of land he's selling,
A syringe, and some dirty papers,
A bawdy-house screw, with box of wafers.

  Then all the shelves she searched around,
Where not one book was to be found;
But gallipots all in a row,
And glistening vials, a fine show!

  What one pot hid she thinks was this:
Diaclom magnum cum gummis,

And spread there was with art, *secundum*
Unguentum neopolitanum;
Pots of pomatum, panacea,
Injections for a gonorrhea;
Of empty ones there were a score,
Of newly filled as many more.
In plenty too stood box of pills,
Nor did there lack for chirurgeon's bills,
Nor nasty rags all stiff with matter,
Nor bottle of mercurial water,
The use of which he does determine
To cure his itch, and kill his vermin:
"Oh heaven!" says she, "what creature's man?
All stink without, and worse within!"

   With that she rose and went away,
For there she could no longer stay;
And scarce she got in the bedchamber,
And thought herself there out of danger,
But quick she heard with both her ears
Strephon come swearing up the stairs;
She swiftly crept behind the screen,
In order not for to be seen.

   Then in came Strephon, lovely sight!
Who had not slept a wink all night;
He staggers in, he swears, he blows,
With eyes like fire, and snotty nose;
A mixture glazed his cheeks and chin
Of claret, snuff, and odious phlegm;
And servant with him, to undress him,
And loving Strephon so caressed him:
"Come hither, Tom, and kiss your master;
Oons, to my groin come put a plaster."

   Tom dexterously his part he played,
To touch his bubo's not afraid;

Nor need he then to hesitate,
But strewed on the precipitate;
Then, in a moment, all the room
Did with the smell of ulcer fume,
And would have lasted very long,
Had not sour belches smelled as strong,
Which from her nose did soon depart,
When overcome with stink of fart,
And after, then came thick upon it
The odious, nauseous one of vomit,
That pour'd out from mouth and nose
Both on his bed, and floor, and clothes;
Nor was it lessened e'er a bit,
Nor overcome, by stink of s—t,
Which, in the pot and round about
The brim and sides, he squirted out;
But when poor Tom pulled off his shoes,
There was a greater stink of toes,
And sure, a nasty, loathsome smell
Must come from feet as black as hell.

Then tossed in bed Tom left his Honour,
And went to call up Peggy Connor
To empty th'pot and mop the room,
To bring up ashes and a broom,
And, after that, most pleasantly
To keep his master company.
The prisoner now being suffocated,
And saw the door was wide dilated,
She thought high time to post away,
For it was ten o'clock i' th' day;
And, ere that she got out of doors,
He turns, farts, hiccups, groans and snores.

Ladies, you'll think 'tis admirable
That this to all men's applicable;
And though they dress in silk and gold,

Could you their insides but behold,
There you fraud, lies, deceit would see,
And pride, and base impiety.
So let them dress the best they can,
They are still fulsome, wretched Man.

Miss W—

*"The Lady's Dressing-Room" was the first of several "excremental" poems written by Swift in his later years. The above riposte was published anonymously in 1732, shortly after the original appeared. It is interesting that an 18th-century woman was able to match (perhaps even outdo) Swift in scatalogical bad taste. Though the author's identity is still unknown, there has been no evidence to suggest that the poem was *not* written by a woman.

Alexander Pope (1688–1744)

Epitaph*

Here lyes John Hughes and Sarah Drew.
Perhaps you'l say, what's that to you?
Believe me Friend much may be said
On this poor Couple that are dead.
On Sunday next they should have marry'd;
But see how oddly things are carry'd.
On Thursday last it rain'd and Lighten'd,
These tender lovers sadly frighten'd
Shelter'd beneath the cocking Hay
In Hopes to pass the Storm away.
But the bold Thunder found them out
(Commission'd for that end no Doubt)
And seizing on their trembling Breath
Consign'd them to the Shades of Death.
Who knows if 'twas not kindly done?
For had they seen the next Year's Sun
A Beaten Wife and Cuckold Swain
Had jointly curs'd the marriage chain.
Now they are happy in their Doom
For P. has wrote upon their Tomb.

Lady Mary Wortley Montagu

*Written in response to two sentimental epitaphs by Pope on a young couple killed by lightning, in which he suggests that the pair would otherwise have lived in blissful harmony.

Verses Address'd to the Imitator of the First Satire of the Second Book of Horace*

In two large Columns, on thy motley Page,
Where *Roman* Wit is strip'd with *English* Rage;
Where Ribaldry to Satire makes pretence;
And modern Scandal rolls with ancient Sense;
Whilst on one side we see how *Horace* thought;
And on the other, how he never wrote:
Who can believe, who view the bad and good,
That the dull Copi'st better understood
That *Spirit,* he pretends to imitate,
Than heretofore that *Greek* he did translate?
  Thine is just such an image of *his* Pen,
As thou thy self art of the Sons of Men:
Where our own Species in Burlesque we trace,
A Sign-Post Likeness of the noble Race;
That is at once Resemblance and Disgrace.
  Horace can laugh, is delicate, is clear;
You, only coarsely rail, or darkly sneer:
His Style is elegant, his Diction pure,
Whilst none thy crabbed Numbers can endure;
Hard as thy Heart, and as thy Birth obscure.
But how should'st thou by Beauty's Force be moved,
No more for loving made, than to be lov'd?
It was the Equity of righteous Heav'n,
That such a Soul to such a Form was giv'n;
And shews the Uniformity of Fate,
That one so odious, shou'd be born to hate.
  When God created Thee, one would believe,
He said the same as to *the snake of Eve;*
To human Race Antipathy declare,
'Twixt them and Thee be everlasting War.
But oh! the Sequel of the Sentence dread,
And whilst you *bruise their Heel,* beware your Head.
  Nor think thy Weakness shall be thy Defence;
The Female Scold's Protection in Offence.

Sure 'tis as fair to beat who cannot fight,
As 'tis to libel those who cannot write.
And if thou drawst thy Pen to aid the Law,
Others a Cudgel, or a Rod, may draw.
   If none with Vengeance yet thy Crimes pursue,
Or give thy manifold Affronts their due;
If Limbs unbroken, Skin without a Stain,
Unwhipt, unblanketed, unkick'd, unslain;
That wretched little Carcass you retain:
The Reason is, not that the World wants Eyes;
But thou'rt so mean, they see, and they despise.
When fretful *Porcupine,* with rancorous Will,
From mounted Back shoots forth a harmless Quill,
Cool the Spectators stand; and all the while,
Upon the angry little Monster smile.
Thus 'tis with thee: —whilst impotently safe,
You strike unwounding, we unhurt can laugh.
Who but must laugh, this Bully when he sees,
A puny Insect shiv'ring at a Breeze?
One over-match'd by ev'ry Blast of Wind,
Insulting and provoking all Mankind.
   Is this the *Thing* to keep Mankind in awe,
To make those tremble who escape the Law?
Is this *the Ridicule* to live so long,
The deathless Satire, and *immortal Song?*
No: like thy self-blown Praise, thy Scandal flies;
And, as we're told of Wasps, it stings and dies.
   If none do yet return th'intended Blow;
You all your Safety to your Dullness owe:
But whilst that Armour thy poor Corps defends,
'Twill make thy Readers few, as are thy Friends;
Those, who thy Nature loath'd, yet lov'd thy Art,
Who lik'd thy Head, and yet abhor'd thy Heart;
Chose thee, to read, but never to converse,
And scorn'd in Prose, him whom they priz'd in Verse.
Even they shall now their partial Error see,
Shall shun thy Writings like thy Company;
And to thy Books shall ope their Eyes no more,

Than to thy Person they wou'd do their Door.
   Nor thou the Justice of the World disown,
That leaves Thee thus an Out-cast, and alone;
For tho' in Law, to murder be to kill,
In Equity the Murder's in the Will:
Then whilst with Coward Hand you stab a Name,
And try at least t'assassinate our Fame;
Like the first bold Assassin's be thy Lot,
Ne'er be thy Guilt forgiven, or forgot;
But as thou hate'st, be hated by Mankind,
And with the Emblem of thy crooked Mind,
Mark'd on thy Back, like *Cain,* by God's own Hand;
Wander like him, accursed through the Land.

Lady Mary Wortley Montagu

*See Pope's "Dunciad" and "Epistle 2. To a Lady," where Lady Mary is referred to as "Sappho."
In others of his poems she is excoriated by name.

   Once a friend, neighbor, and admirer of Lady Mary, Pope later turned the full force of his
venom against her, attacking her in malicious verse and calling her, among other things, a
"whore." His fury, he claimed, was caused by her having borrowed some bedsheets from him,
which she returned unwashed. According to Lady Mary's account, he made a pass at her, and
she, despite her best efforts, was overcome by "an immoderate fit of laughter."

George Lyttleton, 1st Baron Lyttleton (1709–1773)

*A Synopsis of Lord Lyttleton's "Advice to a Lady"**

Be plain in Dress and sober in your Diet;
In short my Dearee, kiss me, and be quiet.

Lady Mary Wortley Montagu

*This response to Lord Lyttleton's poem was originally handwritten on a manuscript copy he had sent to Lady Mary. It is not known whether he ever knew her reaction.

Thomas Gray (1716–1771)

*Response to Thomas Gray by His Favourite Cat, Selima**

It's not my fault the vase's side
Was slipp'ry as an icy slide—
The potter glazed it so;
You bought that hideous Chinese pot,
Filled it with water, fish—for what?
Just fashion's bibelot.

Its colours suited well, I knew,
Flattered my tabby fur which grew
So velvet on my paws;
I saw my plump face mirrored there
(Would human face were half as fair!)
And twitched my purring jaws.

You think I'd steal your precious fish?
I like my food on china dish,
Not dripping from a jar.
I'm not a hunter: get this straight,
I like my cushion, warmth, a plate
Of cream and caviare.

All cats need sleep, perchance to dream;
I grant you such a wat'ry stream
Is dangerous, near;
I blame the fickleness of Fate
Who called too softly, and too late;
I didn't hear.

I popped up eight times from that flood,
Mewing aloud—it did no good:
You're deafer than a post.

You never even moved your head,
Till "Where's my favourite cat?" you said.
Your "favourite"'s now a ghost.

So listen, poet, truth will out:
You're not a "favourite" if your shout
'S ignored and out of place.
True love and favour lies in care—
Like off'ring me your favourite chair.
I rest my case.

D.A. Prince

*See Gray's "Ode on the Death of a Favourite Cat, Drowned in a Tub of Gold Fishes." The form of Prince's poem follows Gray's original.

Oliver Goldsmith (c. 1730–1774)

When Lovely Woman*

When lovely woman wants a favor
  And finds, too late, that man won't bend,
What earthly circumstance can save her
  From disappointment in the end?

The only way to bring him over,
  The last experiment to try,
Whether a husband or a lover,
  If he have feeling is—to cry.

Phoebe Cary

*See Goldsmith's "When Lovely Woman Stoops to Folly."

William Blake (1757–1827)

The Tyger's Reply to Blake*

Meagre, meagre, little man,
Mouth your verses while you can;
Every predator despises
Metaphysical surmises.

Yet I'm forced to ask myself
From what dim and dusty shelf
Did the Source of Being fetch
Such a miserable wretch?

What the pleasure, what the gain?
In what ferment was His brain,
Who after sun and star and cat
Formed so poor a thing as that,

Neither swift nor sage nor good,
Scarcely palatable food?
Yet how impertinently Man
Dares speculate how *I* began!

Mary Holtby

*See Blake's "The Tyger."

From Nobomommy*

Why art thou huffy & peevish,
Brother of certainties?
Why wear thy Father's glower
And stoke his radiant Eyes?

Why wreathed in silence sleeps
A sister in thy lineaments & laws,
Unless she steal the peach
Out of the canny serpent's jaws?
Or dost thou fear the serpent's Teeth
Are bared in Female maws?

Rachel Loden

*See Blake's "To Nobodaddy" and "The Question Answer'd."

Walking a Lobster with Blake along Speedway

Goldbarth says, "Two hundred years earlier, Blake wrote,
'He who desires but acts not breeds pestilence'."
He just leaves it at that. Goldbarth is always fondling
the pagan in him and Jewish law. But I don't want to talk
about Goldbarth here. I want to fall into step with Blake
and quarrel about such toss-offs when dropped into the minds
of the stupid and untutored.

Here we're entering November, your birth month, and I'm
reminded of a woman I loved born the same day who took
it as a sign. How could you know a twit with no mind
would connect up with your mystics? What a pattern
was set jumping to her heat, leaving bodies dropped
along a dead-bloom path.

She thought she was walking with you in Hyde Park
as you leaped from tree to shrub gibbering
Swedenborgian systems. I have a quarrel with you,
Will Blake. She had no judgment, but you ruined
her life with your silly pronouncements.

"Wasn't it Gerard de Nerval (Goldbarth says)—
some symbolist poet—who in a fit of revel
or breakdown walked a lobster on a leash?"

I heard it was a langouste, but what matter,
the man was unbalanced.

Laurel Speer

The Skin of It

> ...And thus I say to little English boy:
> When I from black and he from white cloud free,
> And round the tent of God like lambs we joy,
>
> I'll shade him from the heat till he can bear
> To lean in joy upon our father's knee;
> And then I'll stand and stroke his silver hair,
> And be like him, and he will then love me.
> —Blake, "The Little Black Boy"

She was black,
I was white,
there was always the skin of it,
(though I whispered through the night,
isn't love enough?)
And though I thought I knew the world,
thought they would leave us to each other
my lover was wise, feared
the evening sky would not take us;
(though I whispered through the night,
isn't love enough?)

The Nineteenth-Century Poets

William Wordsworth (1770–1850)

The Solitary Reaper Gets Her Words' Worth*

Behold him, idle dandy there,
Silken shirt and tailored breeches!
Deciding he must stop and stare
And ponder what labor teaches.
Alone I cut and bind the while,
Alone he finds a patch of shade;
On which of us does Fortune smile:
He the man, or I the maid?

I doubt my singing caught his ear;
My work-parched voice is faint and thin.
Chancing to find a lone girl here
Has made him feel more masculine.
My fingers tighten 'round the sickle,
Though his death would be my undoing;
I pray he opts to mount yon hill
And not give himself to wooing.

What does he think this spot may yield:
A wayside rest for weary bands?
'Tis but my father's distant field,
A place I know with calloused hands.
This vale to me's a place for toil:
The only roof's the high blue dome,
The only floor's the rocky soil,
And dreams are useless as a poem.

Alone I cut and bind the grain,
Truly alone, for he has gone;
The sight of work has caused him pain
And made him long to be back home.

Perhaps a maid will bring him tea
And cold compresses for his brow;
And he will sit and think of me
Forever, as I am right now.

Jean LeBlanc

*LeBlanc's poem follows the same form as Wordsworth's "The Solitary Reaper."

Jacob*

He dwelt among "Apartments let,"
  About five stories high;
A man, I thought, that none would get,
  And very few would try.

A boulder, by a larger stone
  Half hidden in the mud,
Fair as a man when only one
  Is in the neighborhood.

He lived unknown, and few could tell
  When Jacob was not free;
But he has got a wife—and O!
  The difference to me!

Phoebe Cary

*See "She Dwelt Among the Untrodden Ways."

An Argument with Wordsworth

> Poetry. . .takes its origins from emotion recollected in tranquility.
> (Preface to the *Lyrical Ballads*)

People are always quoting that and all of them seem to agree
And it's probably most unwise to admit that it's different for me.
I have emotion—no one who knows me could fail to detect it—
But there's a serious shortage of tranquility in which to recollect it.
So this is my contribution to the theoretical debate:
Sometimes poetry is emotion recollected in a highly emotional state.

Wendy Cope

Walter Savage Landor (1775–1864)

Rose Aylmer's Cousin*

"Ah, what avails the sceptered race
   and what the form divine?"
Plenty. Just add a pretty face
and men collapse all over the place
   till forced to stand in line.

Gail White

*See Landor's "Rose Aylmer."

Leigh Hunt (1784–1859)

Jenny to L.H.*

Leigh Hunt kiss'd me when we met,
   Ruck'd the rug and let the cat in;
Golly, but his kiss was wet!
   Trust old creepy to get that in.
Boring fellow drives me mad:
    "Darling, sweetheart, say you've miss'd me!"
How I wish a likelier lad
   Could have kiss'd me....

Mary Holtby

Another Cynical Variation*

Gerald kissed me[1] when he left,
   Just before I put the cat out;[2]
Time, you thief, who are so deft
   In culling sweet things, please leave that out!

Say I'm happy, never bored,[3]
   Say that pain and toil have missed me,[4]
Say I'm young and strong,[5] but Lord!
   Gerald kissed me![1]

[1]On the hand!

[2]Indicating late hour of the evening.

[3]Never?—well—hardly ever.

[4]Untrue.

[5]Not as young and strong as I used to be.

Helen

*See Hunt's "Jenny Kissed Me."

George Gordon, Lord Byron (1788–1824)

from *Death of a Regional Poet**

"As the soil is, so the heart," Byron
  Adds, "of man." I hope he meant women too,
But as he splits the female sex in siren
  Class or artless nymph (And the horrid few
Of intellectual bent and other tirin'
  Tendencies, he saw through specs of blue),
We can't be sure he meant his Byronic heart
To have, in the female, an equal counterpart.

(Canto I, Stanza XXII)
Kathleene West

*The poem uses the ottava rima form of Byron's *Don Juan*.

Donna Julia's First Letter
*After Juan's Departure for Cadiz**

Isabella, more and more I remember childhood
and you lifting your petticoats under the arbor

just to feel the sun on you. It is late summer.
We have finished our studies. The governess sleeps
on the shaded bench surrounded by roses. Remember

what happened next? By now I know you have heard
my story—even you, in the cloisters
where I am going. My choice will end me

there, near God and you, whom I've lied to.
My virtue was so easy all those years

it was safe: a husband too old for much,
my own body trained to forget itself.
And I had grown as good a shrew as any.

I will travel as far within the convent walls
as he, as far as I ever did between my husband's house

and Donna Inez's garden with its trellises,
its fleshy hanging flowers. How she dangled
before me that boy plumping into ripeness,

his rich skin and delicate fingers
like yours—even his eyes, coquette's eyes like yours,

those fabulous lashes shading the danger.
A fan, a veil—what a flirt I could have made him!

It is bad manners for a woman to love
too much, to lose to passion what helps her
button her body in, button her whole self

with steady fingers, bind up silk and lace,
button after button, her head lowered,
her lashes lowered over her eyes, working

in perfect containment. Now I will walk in
from the stifling sun to that labyrinth of cells,
the stone walls everywhere cool and damp.

I will reach out to the stones' caress.
I will press my body against them, there

in the cool, almost darkness of midday.
I will cultivate the habit, draw its folds
down over my shoulders; bare

and mobile all day under rough cloth
my nipples will grow tender then raw

with passion; I will know
the feel of this flesh, the life I take
in my own hands all night. Bella,

and I will end well! When I finish this
I am ready. I will write him

on gilt-edged paper, with the seal
I use for you—*elle vous suit partout*—
the right lies about a woman's one love

and passion, a lady's diminutive tragedy.
My last decorous act, which he may let go
to whatever wind he pleases. Bella, no tears.

Katharine Coles

*In Byron's *Don Juan,* Donna Julia, age 23 and married to a much older man, falls in love with
16-year-old Juan. After her husband discovers them together, Juan flees and Julia enters a con-
vent. Her parting letter to him (Canto I, Stanzas CXCII–CXCVII) includes the famous passage:
"Man's love is of man's life a thing apart, / 'Tis woman's whole existence. . . ."

Poets and Peacocks

"Love hurts" and sometimes there's no cure for it
but death or amputation. Byron said,
"Man's love is of man's life a thing apart,
'Tis woman's whole existence"! He was wrong:
he should have watched her suckling her lover's son.
"Love changes everything"—but so does time;
for although Shakespeare said, "Love's not Time's fool,"
frequent separations wear it thin.

"All you need is love": well, it is true
whatever else we need, we need love most.
Are human beings alone in their desire
to pass their genes on to the sound of music,
sometimes, moodily subsuming sex itself
within a predilection for poetry?
Or is it just another courtship ploy
like the peacock's gorgeous fanned-out feathers?
Is man's pontification about love
meant simply as a monumental turn-on,
and "*amor vincit omnia*" just Nature's plan:
feathers for peacocks, poetry for men?

Margaret Rogers

Percy Bysshe Shelley (1792–1822)

Shelley's Death

> Killing the sense with passion
> —"Epipsychidion"

Shelley set out that day
on the lightest craft,
on slender laths of wood
opposed moods of an iron sea,
idling that morning like silk,
by noon, shattering.

Sailor, slack hand and sheet
but a moment, necessarily,
to drink wine, eat fruit, look around,
and mechanical weather
is on you, a crushing gear,
before you can reef or come about.

Sails skim down,
struck sodden, pull;
boom, spar, mast
slice water that slides back
as though nothing
had gone through or passed.

The gunnel tips like a cup
at the mouth; thirst
deluged till it is sunk
in exaggeration or floats absurdly
as a dipper in a vat.
Among seawrack Shelley was found.

Smoke rose
like many sails
from the dark beach,
an armada of desires
spiraling, his understanding
consumed.

Judith Bishop

Mary's Present

I'm not believing for a minute Shelley's heart
wouldn't burn. He'd drowned, that was clear.
His body washed up with a friend after two weeks.
Italian law decreed fire for stench and disease.
Friends obliged. It was a task. They had time
to think, while smoke and odors breezed the beach.
Trelawny says a seabird crossed and re-crossed
the fire, riding the heat. Trelawny was there.
He claims the heart sat at the center leaking oils,
so he fished it out. What about Williams, the other?
Falling to pieces heart and bowels, while Trelawny
gripped his burnt palm? Mary got it. Wonderful.
She put it in a box? Her closet? In a jar
next to the plums? Stunning.

Laurel Speer

To Percy, from ____*

My state's been too often explained
   For me to explain it;
And feelings—I must say I'm pained,
   And why should I feign it?
I really do think it's unfair:

A bit of the other,
And what in the end do you care
   If I end up a mother?

OK then, don't call it "love"
   If the word seems affected,
But frankly, when push comes to shove,
   There's no doubt I'm rejected.
The desire of a girl for a ring
   Is the cause of my sorrow;
Don't try to make light of your fling,
   But buy it tomorrow!

Mary Holtby

*See Shelley's "To ___," beginning, "One word is too often profaned / For me to profane it."

Sonnet to Percy in Italy, from England*

I cannot come to your quaint Italy,
Not at this hour, when one can plainly see
that your impatience far outweighs your heart
And makes such issue of alone, apart.
But can one help but wonder, Percy Bysshe,
If you mistake mere momentary wish,
Construe a candle's temporary flame
To be such fiery "love," it has no name?
To me, affection does not weigh a feather
That can be lost on differences in weather,
Disparity of language, dress or hair,
While fireflies flash here happily as there.
Sir, you will have to hope against scant hope;
So do as your Italians do, and cope.

June Owens

*See Shelley's "To Maria Gisborne in England, from Italy."

John Clare (1793–1864)

John Clare

John Clare, I cried last night
For you—your grass-green coat,
Your oddness, others' spite,
Your fame, enjoyed and lost,
Your gift, and what it cost.

Awake in the early hours
I heard you with my eyes,
Carolling woods and showers.
As if a songbird's throat
Could utter words, you wrote.

I listened late and long—
Each clear, true, loving note
Placed justly in its song.
Sometimes for sheer delight,
John Clare, I cried last night.

Wendy Cope

John Keats (1795–1821)

*The Bride of Quietness**

My husband, when he *was* my husband, possessed
Electrifying energy, humor,
The vital heat of violent force compressed...
Contraries in a controlling frame. Few more

Creative and compelling men could fire
The clay I scarcely dared to call my soul.
Shapeless, lacking properties of higher
Existence, it was perfect for the mold

He cast me in: classic receptacle,
A thing for use but full of elegance,
An ode to Greece, forever practical,
Tellingly patterned with the hunt and dance.

My lines were lies; and yet he seemed to see
Aesthetic validation in my form.
I asked him not to draw away from me.
He said he feared he might commit some harm—

Some accidental, inadvertent hurt—
And shatter in an instant all the love
He'd poured out in the effort to convert
My ordinary mind to a work of

Art. And how he shuddered if I assumed
A new position or a point of view!
As if I were a royal vase entombed
After the ancient style, and the issue

Of my movement could only be a change
In where he stood, relative to his wife.

I must perdure inanimate and strange
And still, if he would justify his life.

For I was the object of his most profound
Research, the crafty subject of his thesis,
And all I had to do to bring him down
Was let my heart break into all those pieces

It ached to break into in any case.
Upon his graduation, when the guests
Had gone, and night was settling on his face,
Raising my voice above his dreams I confessed

That beauty held no truth for me, nor truth
Beauty, but I was made as much of earth
As I had been, barbaric and uncouth,
Enjoined to rhythm, shiftings, blood and birth,

And void of principle. He said he'd father
No children. I could hardly help knowing
That he'd be wrong to trust me any farther.
By sunrise it was clear he would be going

Soon. Now from time to time I see him here
And there. The shoulders have gone slack, the eyes
Conduct a lesser current and I fear
That when they catch me spying, it's no surprise

To him. He always found poetic justice
Amusing, and he knows I wait my turn.
The artist dies; but what he wrought will last
Forever, when I cradle his cold ashes in this urn.

Kelly Cherry

*See Keats's "Ode on a Grecian Urn."

Lamia to Lycius*

> "A serpent!" echoed he; no sooner said
> than with a frightful scream she vanishèd
> and Lycius' arms were empty of delight,
> as were his limbs of life, from that same night.

Do you hear me, Lycius? Do you hear these dreams
moving like words out of the air, it seems?
Did I really eat the feast and fill your arms?
Have you found my picture grace painted on lies, not charms?
You think you saw me thin into a ghost,
impaled by his old eyes, with their shuddering boast
of pride that kills truth with philosophy.
But you hear this voice. Is it a serpent's, or
is it a woman's, this rich-emblazoned core
reaching out loud for you, as I once reached
for you with my two hands, and your whole life beseeched?
I had a woman's eyes, that cried such tears
my serpent body broke, and woman's teeth
that never bit, although the ruddy wreath
of my soft lips was closing. But my heart
crawled like a serpent, and that is the part
you married, Lycius, when you made the sun
shine over my damp earth, and grew with me to one.
I had thought our love was stronger than belief,
close enough to absorb such stinging grief!
But now I am all serpent, and I go
where serpents go, taking my path, as slow
as any creature fallen to the earth—
though I will flash with somber fire mirth
through this volcano belly when you come near,
till every human word you say is clear.

Annie Finch

*Lamia, in Keats's poem of the same name, is a serpent who takes the form of a beautiful
woman. She and Lycius fall in love, but at their wedding her true nature is revealed, whereupon
Lamia vanishes and Lycius dies. In ancient mythology a lamia was a monster in female form who
preyed upon human beings.

La Belle Dame sans Merci Offers Her Version

So what! bewailing last night's charms,
Hung-over, pale and muttering;
The weather's bleak, so are the words
You're uttering.

We had a good day out, we two,
Sang Dylan hits, "Times Are A-changing";
You showed a talent rare and sweet
For flower-arranging.

I cooked you supper late last night;
Not Cordon Bleu, though, I admit;
Still, roots and manna, honey too—
You finished it.

And then slept badly? Gluttons do.
Ask yourself this solemn question:
Are your damp brow and pallor mere
Indigestion?

Please save your dreams for analysts;
Spare me; give fantasies no tongue;
They'll say your one-night stand's to blame,
Will Freud and Jung.

The morning-after has one cure
To ease the aching clasp you're in:
This pill will bring your colour back—
An aspirin.

D.A. Prince

Henry Wadsworth Longfellow (1807–1882)

Bad Little Girl

There was a little girl
Who had a little curl
Right in the middle of her forehead;
And when she was good
She was very, very good,
But when she was bad she wrote poetry.

Toni La Ree Bennett

Edgar Allen Poe (1809–1849)

Annabel Lee Does a Post-Mortem on the Hazards of Romance with a Metrical Poet

When I told him my name was Annabel Lee
his face lit up like a Christmas tree.
I could see rhymes swirling through his head
and might have known I'd wind up dead
like Ulalume and that weird Lenore—
I should have been shrieking NEVERMORE!
but his verse rolled on like the sounding sea
as we strolled and the cold enfolded me.
What carried me off? It was not pneumonia
but simply a case of acute euphonia.

Joyce La Mers

To Mr. Poe, From His Beautiful Annabel Lee

My dear Mr. Poe, you silly twit, to sleep so by the sea!
I'm dead, you're not, and that is why it's over between you and me.
Get a house in town, get a job, clear your head;
Get dressed, comb your hair, find a girl who's not dead
                    Like your beautiful Annabel Lee.

We loved, it is true, and we walked by the sea.
We walked and we walked and we walked, didn't we?
Angels didn't much envy our romance, my twitness,
They envied the cardiovascular fitness
                    Of your beautiful Annabel Lee.

Ed, I hated that beach, the sand and the sun
(The moon by the time you and I were quite done
Walking that beach in the rain and the wind).
Bedraggled, I'd wallow; you'd breathe deep and grin.
       "You're beautiful, Annabel Lee."

Oh, it's true we were children; we walked by the sea.
It's true, I loved you and I guess you loved me.
True, you pointed to stars, to the moon, to the tides.
Still, I wish you'd had *something* to tell me besides
       "You're beautiful, Annabel Lee."

But now that I'm dead, you're walking no more.
You're balding, you're fat, and you've started to snore.
I look down from this heaven, and I must confide
I'm glad I have left what you're sleeping beside—
       The body of Annabel Lee.

Are you happier now that I've not much to say?
I'm consistently pretty—don't have a bad day.
It's your favorite dress and my hair is arranged—
Come to think of it, Eddie, not too much has changed
       For beautiful Annabel Lee.

And I'm so glad to know our souls won't be "dissevered,"
(While you sleep with my body)—you're ever so clever.
Poor Annabel Lee, you've bedazzled, bedeviled her.
But I guess I was always a roll in the sepulchre.
       Signed, beautiful Annabel Lee.

Gray Davis

To Edgar, from Helen*

Edgar, your verses are to me
  An irremediable bore:
I can't think what their point may be

Nor why you made the effort, nor
   Quite what you take me for.

How desperately you seem to comb
  The classics for a hopeful case
As far as possible from home.
  And your rhymes are a disgrace,
And you write a lousy pome.

Now things have got to such a pitch
   I really don't know where I stand:
   Psyche—an ostrich in the sand;
Helen—a calculating bitch…
   Let both be banned!

Mary Holtby

*See Poe's "To Helen."

Alfred, Lord Tennyson (1809–1892)

Domestic Scenes from Lady Tennyson's Journal*

When the days are warm and our island
is green, we have our tea
in the garden under the chestnut tree.
After tea, you take your nap beside
the strawberry bed while I sit and watch you.
At night, you read to me. It helps me
to sleep. It helps me to be quiet,
when the days are warm and our island

> is green.
> A beetle in our room
> stares at me with bright mean
> eyes. You put him outside
> in the dark where he can't be seen.

Some days we walk the path to the sea.
If the day is windy, the sea
hurls its salt sparay against the white cliffs. We take
our boys fishing and Lionel catches
a fish, green-gold with a streak
of red. At home you soak in a tub.
I want to lift your damp curls, touch
the soft hollow in your neck.

> While outside
> Cockneys are everywhere.
> Some of them even hide
> behind our hedge. They try
> to spy on us inside.

One day there is a robin in our room.
While you read to me, the robin sits
near us by the fire and brings a bit

of spring into the room. It is too cold
to go outside today. Our boys stamp
the snow from their boots and come inside.
The sun goes down. Snow piles high beside
the gate posts and the wind drives drifts against

                    our door. The night
                    is still, An owl hoots.
                    The robin hops on the floor.
                    And you read to me
                    about the London poor.

Margaret Kay

*Emily Tennyson married the poet when she was thirty-seven, after fourteen years of hesitation on both sides. However, she promptly became the perfect poet's wife, capably managing their finances, correspondence, children, entertaining, and two households; shielding Tennyson from unwanted visitors and other distractions; serving as resident sounding-board for his work in progress; recording in her journal their daily activities. In the twenty-fifth year of their marriage, she suffered a sudden nervous collapse and remained a semi-invalid for the rest of her life. She never resumed her journal.

Penelope and Ulysses Settle a Domestic Dispute*

(Tennyson Revisited)

She'd managed on her own for 20 years,
Had raised his son and seen the crops safe in.
But then one day he drifted home again
Weary and old, and full of jealous fears.
His body, scarred by battles not her own,
Had lain with Circe, so the rumor said.
She really didn't want him in her bed—
Grizzled and toothless, aging skin and bone,
Not like the sweet young men who'd filled her days
With dark excitement, eager for her nod…
All slaughtered! Had he thought that she'd applaud?
She screamed across the scene that shocked her gaze,
"Go sail beyond the sunset! I can't stand you!"
And so he sailed, pretending he had planned to.

Joyce La Mers

*See Tennyson's "Ulysses" and also (in this volume) "The Wife of the Man of Many Wiles," a response to Homer by A.E. Stallings.

Robert Browning (1812–1889)

A Browning Toccata*

Robert Browning, weighty poet, this is very strange to find
All these words and all these pictures, yet I never see defined
Any woman at the centre of the stage you call your mind.

Poor *Last Duchess* from Ferrara, mute in paint on palace walls,
Silenced by a husband's orders, cold as wind through winter halls,
Did you ever hear her whispers, shyer than the cricket's calls?

Famous painters, worthy bishops, oh, you let them have their say;
You could always hear the man's voice, justified in every way.
Did you think, perhaps in secret, women's words were merely play?

Any wife to any husband—there's the line men want to hear;
Patient, passive, husband-centred, letting maleness domineer.
Did no woman send *you* packing, with proverbial flea in ear?

How you crammed your life with writing. Did you listen?—never once.
Dust and ashes, dead and done with; if you'd known what woman wants
You'd have scored out lines, whole poems, known yourself an empty dunce.

From the Casa Guidi casements, high above the Florence streets,
Did you never hear the gossip, feel the women's throbbing beats
As they cackled sex and childbirth, death and marriage, men's defeats?

As your poems in their volumes, born in the Victorian age,
In your time they had some glory, now they curl and show their age;
What of art is left, I wonder, now that women earn a wage?

Dark Elizabeth who loved you—she's the one whose verses last,
Speaking through impassioned sonnets, nailing proud love to her mast.
Loved today and still as living, not a relic in the past.

Robert Browning, bound by rhythm, even when your subject's gone,
Did you never scan your future, wince at reputation wan,
But expect your adulation to go on, and on, and on?

D.A. Prince

*See Browning's "A Toccata of Galuppi's."

"My Last Duchess" Responds to Robert Browning

Night after night he didn't satisfy
but entered fierce and hard, old bull in rut
without one word of love. Sometimes I'd cry
as Renaissance man quelled his appetite
like a prize rooster favoring some hen
by sharing items on his pedigree.
Had for the dowry, murdered in my teens,
I ask revenge not metric poetry.

Sometimes I'd almost laugh, though, at the bag
that kept his bloodline safe beneath a flap
of tissue stallions share with gelded nags
and God with male poets who write crap.

"Frà Pandolf's hands / Worked busily a day"
to paint my soul, to introduce foreplay.

Joanne Seltzer

Porphyria's Reply*

Bobby, my love, you guessed not how
My darling one wish would be heard:
(Tedious to give the background, now
That every detail has occurred
Precisely in the way preferred.)
How should a girl of gumption fail
With one so gullible, so vain?
What true romantic could refrain
From such an apt response to pain?
And now, as fearfully you wait
In God's strange silence that I share,
I hear the creaking of the gate
And know their part who gather there:
You too lie strangled in my hair.

Mary Holtby

---

*See Browning's "Porphyria's Lover," a monologue in which the speaker of the poem, in response to Porphyria's wish to belong to him forever, strangles her with her long hair.

Edward Lear (1812–1888)

Edward Lear

> He weeps by the side of the ocean,
>   He weeps on the top of the hill;
> He purchases pancakes and lotion,
>   And chocolate shrimps from the mill.
>   —"How Pleasant to Know Mr. Lear!"

Never can one choose to be
a laureate of restlessness—
and yet we speak a language

with hardly the tipsiest
raft to float upon.
And if at night birds perch

on our topmost hats
our favorite must be
a quivery celestial jelly.

How do we rest upon our little
bobbing rafts? Now a dust
the color of shrimp

lights our rooms. These moments grow
each to each suddenly
precarious

in a summer
when we are turning
to the end of a century

when there's no hill,
no ocean,
no weeping without purchases.

Lee Upton

Walt Whitman (1819–1892)

The Language of the Brag

I have wanted excellence in the knife-throw,
I have wanted to use my exceptionally strong and accurate arms
and my straight posture and quick electric muscles
to achieve something at the center of a crowd,
the blade piercing the bark deep,
the haft slowly and heavily vibrating like the cock.

I have wanted some epic use for my excellent body,
some heroism, some American achievement
beyond the ordinary for my extraordinary self,
magnetic and tensile, I have stood by the sandlot
and watched the boys play.

I have wanted courage, I have thought about fire
and the crossing of waterfalls, I have dragged around

my belly big with cowardice and safety,
my stool black with iron pills,
my huge breasts oozing mucus,
my legs swelling, my hands swelling,
my face swelling and darkening, my hair
falling out, my inner sex
stabbed again and again with terrible pain like a knife.
I have lain down.

I have lain down and sweated and shaken
and passed blood and feces and water and
slowly alone in the center of a circle I have
passed the new person out
and they have lifted the new person free of that
language of blood like praise all over the body.

I have done what you wanted to do, Walt Whitman,
Allen Ginsberg, I have done this thing,
I and the other women this exceptional
act with the exceptional heroic body,
this giving birth, this glistening verb,
and I am putting my proud American boast
right here with the others.

Sharon Olds

Walt Whitman Encounters the Cosmos with the Cats of New York

The cats of morning awaken, sultry and feral,
Ready to hunt, to mate, to kick some serious cat butt.
Their green and yellow eyes burst open as a child slits the top off a pumpkin.

The alley cat is awake; the garbage can, last night's refuge, is rudely
        up-ended.
The Vanderbilts' cat awakens on Vanderbilt's pillow.
It washes its face with a loud shlurping noise.
The Vanderbilts do nothing; they are terrified of the thing.
The farm cat is up and about, looking for breakfast;
It falls on the field mice like Basil the Bulgar-Slayer.
The actress's cat makes a nest in last night's costume.
It may as well go back to sleep. She won't be up
Until God knows when. The banker's cat is curled
In a neat little package; it purrs that interest is rising.
The mother cat moves her kittens from the back of the closet
To the fireplace, thinks better of it, moves half of them back,
Then sits in the hallway and says to hell with this motherhood business.

Bastet is walking the streets and I walk with her.
I, Walt Whitman, companion of cats, have become all cats.
I look behind the restaurants for scraps of fish.
I rub myself on the legs of total strangers;

They run off screaming. They are unaware of my secret.
My brothers and sisters and I are watching the East;
The sun only rose this morning
Because my people are watching.

Gail White

Am Lit

So Emily sat with her brother Walt
in the spreading sycamore shade
and each noticed the mottled bark
and the pattern the sunlight made
on the grass

and Walt picked a blade
leaning on one elbow,
his soft shirt open at the throat
the gold hairs curling sweetly on the backs of his wrists
and he rhapsodized on grass, he riffed,
he invented the stiffened white tongue's nearest jazz
democracy's own clamorous voice flowing
with passionate precision
out of his warm red throat

and Emily
in white
close-buttoned
listened
saying nothing
noting
in that grass
a narrow fellow.

Susan Blackwell Ramsey

Matthew Arnold (1822–1888)

That Ghastly Night in Dover*

The sea was calm, and sweet was the night air,
but what a bore! One whiff of ocean breeze
started him blathering all night long, I swear—
stuff about naked shingles and Sophocles.

Katherine McAlpine

*See Arnold's "Dover Beach."

Dante Gabriel Rossetti (1828–1882)

Rossetti's Wife*

He wants his poems, now: the ones he buried
with me, to be a sacrifice of love
forever. There you are: that's being married
to genius. That's what you're dreaming of,

you silly girls who think it was great luck
to rise from milliner to painter's model
to poet's wife. You marry and you're stuck.
Give me an artist for a man who'll coddle

himself. Oh, he's in love with his ideal
and thinks it's you, but it's his bag of tricks—
even when I was dying, he could feel
that I'd be perfect for his Beatrix.

And then? They're all alike, poet or hack—
he digs you up and grabs his verses back.

Gail White

*Elizabeth Siddal Rossetti's distinctive beauty made her an archetype for the Pre-Raphaelite painters. When she died (from an overdose of laudanum), her husband did indeed bury his poems with her, change his mind some years later, and have her body exhumed so he could retrieve them.

Thomas Hardy (1840–1928)

Thoughts of the Woman Much Missed*

No, husband, that was not me calling you, calling you.
The daisies grow above my grave and I
am silent now, the way you wanted me to
be in life. Don't expect a reply.

You did not want to hear my voice when we
were home alone (not even when I wore
the air-blue gown). You expected me to be
silent at table and behind the bedroom door.

So I sat in silence while you danced to the strain
of the Blue Danube Waltz with your lady
literary friend. I was ill and in pain,
but once again I kept silent when you left me

to walk about the streets of London and eye
the young girls there. No, husband, that was not me
calling you, calling you. I am content to lie
beneath the daisies now, quite silently.

Margaret Kay

*See Hardy's "The Voice." The speaker of Kay's poem and the following one is Hardy's first
wife, Emma. After her death, he was overcome with remorse for their unhappy marriage, clung
to her personal possessions as sacred relics, and poured out dozens of love poems in her mem-
ory. This obsession greatly annoyed his young second wife, Florence, typist and nominal author
of a "biography" actually written by Hardy himself. Florence got her revenge, after his death, by
eliminating from the book virtually every positive reference to Emma and consigning all relics
of her to a massive bonfire. The two wives now lie side by side in a Stinsford churchyard along
with Hardy's heart. The rest of him, in ashes, resides in Westminster Abbey.

Emma's Evensong

Cleaving, I call,—no longer bright-souled;
Calling, calling from churchyard and down,
Ghostly frail in a faded blue gown.
Nut-brown has silvered, coarse and cold;

Tears plough my cheeks, furrowed and lined.
Sadly, you noticed what age has wrought
Bearing the conflicts our tensions brought;
Yet, public confessions you declined.

Rose-flush has faded to tombstone gray
Slate like the stones of our waterfall,
Wet from full-lipped kisses,—I recall!
Knowing your elegies, now I pray:

       Let us only remember
       April's eyes of desiring.
Together our hearts in a lone bed lying
       Bury our dark Decembers.

Anita Wintz

Thomas Hardy, Under Glass*

What count of pebbles fits into an urn?
The urn will tell how many or how few;
A cat will know which of her kittens mew,
While we examine Nature's tiniest turn.

Perhaps we delve too deeply, try to learn
By means so miniscule we miss the blue
Investiture of one bright bead of dew
And, missing that and finding naught, we yearn.

But what's more magnifying than a kiss?
Have we to question every blade of grass
And all things measure under microscopes?

I am a simple soul and so think this:
Love is the lens that sees the heart, the glass
Through which Man dreams and ultimately hopes.

June Owens

*See Hardy's "I Look into My Glass."

Stéphane Mallarmé (1842–1898)

*To Mallarmé**

The lamp,
the blank paper,
my elbow under a dream,
the window confronts me,
my images "brise marine,"
exoticisms beyond today.

"Musician of silence,"
when the glass is green with midnight
and rain dripping on tin
takes all conviction from me,

I go away and quarrel
with you, mediator of the void;
go to the most extreme
antiphonies
of rhetoric, unable
to be less than grim.

How speak of unimportance
to define
what should have been?

Deceiver, your lines
have no answer,
your mistress indifference.

Judith Bishop

*"*Brise Marine*" is the title of a poem by Mallarmé. "Musician of silence" is from the poem
"*Sainte*," as translated by Roger Fry.

Robert Bridges (1844–1930)

*for Robert Bridges**

All women born are so diverse
No man should miss their charms assessing
If nothing more, it's worth the search:
All women born are so diverse
From Adam sliced, they do converse
Though seldom speak without digressing
All women born are so diverse
No man should miss their charms assessing.

Anita Wintz

*Bridges's original, also a triolet, begins, "All women born are so perverse / No man need boast their love possessing."

Gerard Manley Hopkins (1844–1889)

On Beria's Lap*

> My childhood was a happy time, a paradise of sorts.
> —Svetlana Peters (Stalin)

> Lana Peters, 66, has wound up in Ladbroke Grove, living in a
> charity hospital for those suffering severe emotional problems.
> —*The Daily Mail* (London)

Svetlana, are you grieving
Over dacha-days unleaving?
Papochka rocked you, kissed you,
Called you mistress
Of the manor, little
Sparrow, obeyed your orders
(And no others) between the trials
And the murders. My Kremlin
Princess! Now you are old and
(They say) bitter. But
In the picture it is summer:
A garden table strewn
With papers, Papochka working
At his business; and you
On Uncle Larya's lap, a little
Shy, a little restless. His eyes
Are blank, his glasses
Glitter. You don't climb
Down, you enter history. It is
The blight that you were born for,
It is a century you mourn for.

Rachel Loden

*Author's note: "Lavrenty Beria, in Stalin's USSR, had more blood on his hands than anyone,
with the exception of Stalin." See Hopkins's "Spring and Fall."

Pied Untidy*

Glory be to God for dappled things—
Except for table-linen stained with wine,
For carpets puddled by the family pup,
Wooden tables circled with white rings,
Lush lawns, pale-patched, that tree roots undermine
And wall-paper that's marked half the way up.

All things spotted, splashed, off-centre, out-of-true;
Whatever's soiled, spoiled, dull where it should shine,
Like a dusty, dirty, tarnished silver cup—
This dappling's the devil's work we must undo:
      Curse him!

Margaret Rogers

*See Hopkins's "Pied Beauty."

A.E. Housman (1859–1936)

*Observation by a Formerly Rose-Lipt Maiden**

At the lads who were lightfoot
  I've taken a look:
What's too broad for leaping
  Just isn't the brook.

Joyce La Mers

*See Housman's "With Rue My Heart Is Laden."

The Shropshire Lad's Fiancee

Since, as you most justly say,
life will pass too soon away,
and our youth, like summer's rose,
scarcely comes before it goes,
let us lie then, head by head,
love and death upon one bed.

In each bed we lie upon
I embrace your skeleton,
and in your changing skin I see
the enduring skull that is to be.
Heart to heart and face to face,
I foresee our last embrace,
dull as Milton's self could wish,
sexless as two sightless fish.

If you think that I should not
be talking such infernal rot,
think, my dearest, it's the way
you talked to me the other day.

Gail White

The Lads of the Village*

The lads of the village, we read in the lay,
By medalled commanders are muddled away,
And the picture that the poet makes is not very gay.

Poet, let the red blood flow, it makes the pattern better,
And let the tears flow, too, and grief stand that is their begetter,
And let man have his self-forged chain and hug every fetter.

For without the juxtaposition of muddles, medals and clay,
Would the picture be so very much more gay,
Would it not be a frivolous dance upon a summer's day?

Oh sigh no more: Away with the folly of commanders.
That will not make a better song upon the field of Flanders,
Or upon any field of experience where pain makes patterns the poet
    slanders.

Stevie Smith

*See the Housman poem beginning, "The lads in their hundreds to Ludlow come in from the fair...."

Rudyard Kipling (1865–1936)

The Feminine "If"

If you can wait on those who'll keep *you* waiting
  And lie to them their own convenient lies,
Or being hated, while reciprocating
  Hide hatred in your heart with smiling eyes:
If you can talk small talk when they desert you,
  Or walk unlimping when you need a crutch;
If friends are foes, and careful neighbours skirt you,
  If others pity you ("Do keep in touch!"),
If you can reach Fate's rotten wheel and spin it
  But lack the courage then to cut and run,
Yours is the female Hell—and once you're in it,
  Don't wonder what it's like to be a nun.

Mary Holtby

William Butler Yeats (1865–1939)

Adam's Curse Revisited

> I said, "A line will take us hours maybe;
> Yet if it does not seem a moment's thought,
> Our stitching and unstitching has been naught.
> Better go down upon your marrow-bones
> And scrub a kitchen pavement, or break stones
> Like an old pauper, in all kinds of weather;
> For to articulate sweet sounds together
> Is to work harder than all these, and yet
> Be thought an idler by the noisy set
> Of bankers, schoolmasters, and clergymen
> The martyrs call the world…"
> —"Adam's Curse"

So Master William has decreed the stitching
of words to be harder than anything
else the rest of us may work to do. Harder
than, day after day, pounding rocks to shards
so that one may eat. Harder, indeed, than
leading flat, slow minds to think or even
to care to think. Harder than salvaging
the souls of intractable tyrants, thieves,

and secret non-believers. And if he
were here today, I'm sure he would agree
it to be harder than singly raising
a family on minimum wage in, say,
Chicago or east L.A. For heaven
knows what he must have known of unchosen
tedium, blisters, and sweat, what with all
that rowing to and fro that far lake isle

of Innisfree. I'm sure, if he could, he'd further
address those of us who know both a word's

needling prick and the heft of a hammer's
shaft. In fact, if it weren't for the roaring flicker
of some club's evening fire and the hushed steam
of his brandy mug, I think I could almost hear him
say, *What makes you think, you noisy idlers,*
that you can both shape and stitch the world?

Debra Pennington

*Leda**

> Ah! Would that the human race
> might bring a curse on the gods!"
> —Euripides, *Hippolytus*

Exactly
fourteen years and
three days
old,
Leda
stood up
in the garden.

With a slight concussion,
one black eye,
three cracked ribs,
a compound fracture of the radius,
and severe multiple lacerations and contusions in the neck
thigh and
abdominal areas,
she
pulled
herself out of
the shrubbery.

There was nothing to reach up to.

Bent double,
gingerly,
hands on the earth,
she pushed herself
away,
up,
until she was
straight again,
until she blotted out a piece of the sky
with her undeniable
outline,
insisting on negative space.

Every bruise where the wings had struck
sang;
where the beak had come down like a fist,
each broken bone belted out
call and response.

Her head was
light from the fracture,
the crack in her skull
where she hit the ground
upon impact.

But holding on
to nothing,
Leda
stood
up
in the garden and
walked
back
to the palace, and
she did not sway,
knowing
exactly
the extent of her injuries,

two blue eggs
already forming inside her;

in the hedge
she
left behind
fistfuls of
bloody white feathers.

Chanda J. Glass

*See Yeats's "Leda and the Swan."

A New Prayer for Daughters

> O may she live like some green laurel
> Rooted in one dear perpetual place.
> . . . . .
> And may her bridegroom bring her to a house
> Where all's accustomed, ceremonious....
> —"A Prayer for My Daughter"

When I was a child there were no towers
for fathers to pace atop and curse storms.
My parents' house did not keep out the rain.
Our lives were battlefields on which we were
opposed by enemies we could not name.
I am not alone in this; many friends
grew up amid such wars. We were taught lies:
the goodness of giving of ourselves is
a gift we ourselves do not deserve, or
that anger is some forbidden fruit we
will be punished for putting to our lips.
The storm into which you were born was not
a storm but full-fledged war; this is life, then,
a war waged by those who are war-weary.

You are not weary, and those of us who
hide our scars envy you your smooth skin of
many colors, your inner confidence.
What is it that you know that you will not
tell your elders? How did you learn of the
volcano that rages within your heart,
whose power you have channeled to your eyes
that you may know danger when you see it;
whose force you have stored in your legs and arms;
and with whose fire you forged your spirit
that, faced with darkness, you may shine brightly,
laugh and cry and fight—the essence of life?
And now you are a woman. Through you I
can sometimes glimpse the raw power of life—
but you have more to do than act my eyes.
You are aware. That is your protection,
that is your gift: awareness. The precious
sense of the rawness of life and the good
that may be had despite ongoing war—
this is what we long for, those of us born blind.
You have your own balance to strike between
rejection, affirmation, war and peace,
between the lives your life will touch and those
whom you will choose to keep as strangers.
Uproot the laurel then, or leave it be
and uproot yourself from the shadow of
the hidden tree. Reject the bridegroom's house,
the noose of custom and ceremony.
Born with awareness, daughters of the world,
with fire within, your vision is your own.

Jean LeBlanc

Gelett Burgess (1866–1951), et al.

from *Diversions of the Re-Echo Club*

> It is with pleasure that we announce our ability to offer to the
> public the papers of the Re-Echo Club. . . . On the occasion of the
> meeting of which the following gems of poesy are the result, the
> several members of the club engaged to write up the well-known
> tradition of the Purple Cow in more elaborate form than the qua-
> train made famous by Mr. Gelett Burgess.

Mr. John Milton:

Hence, vain, deluding cows.
  The herd of folly, without colour bright,
  How little you delight,
  Or fill the Poet's mind, or songs arouse!
  But, hail! thou goddess gay of feature!
  Hail, divinest purple creature!
  Oh, Cow, thy visage is too bright
To hit the sense of human sight.
  And though I'd like, just once, to see thee,
  I never, never, never'd be thee!

Mr. P. Bysshe Shelley:

    Hail to thee, blithe spirit!
      Cow thou never wert;
    But in life to cheer it
      Playest thy full part
In purple lines of unpremeditated art.

    We look before and after
      At cattle as they browse;
    Our most hearty laughter

Something sad must rouse.
Our sweetest songs are those that tell of Purple Cows.

Mr. W. Wordsworth:

She dwelt among the untrodden ways
  Beside the springs of Dee;
A Cow whom there were few to praise
  And very few to see.

A violet by a mossy stone
  Greeting the smiling East
Is not so purple, I must own,
  As that erratic beast.

She lived unknown, that Cow, and so
  I never chanced to see;
But if I had to be one, oh,
  The difference to me!

Mr. T. Gray:

The curfew tolls the knell of parting day,
  The lowing herd winds slowly o'er the lea;
I watched them slowly wend their weary way,
  But, ah, a Purple Cow I did not see.
Full many a cow of purplest ray serene
  Is haply grazing where I may not see;
Full many a donkey writes of her, I ween,
  But neither of these creatures would I be.

Lord A. Tennyson:

Ask me no more. A cow I fain would see
  Of purple tint, like to a sun-soaked grape—

Of purple tint, like royal velvet cape—
But such a creature I would never be—
            Ask me no more.

Mr. J. Keats:

A cow of purple is a joy forever.
Its loveliness increases. I have never
Seen this phenomenon. Yet ever keep
A brave lookout; lest I should be asleep
When she comes by. For, though I would not be one,
I've oft imagined 'twould be joy to see one.

Mr. D.G. Rossetti:

The Purple Cow strayed in the glade;
   (Oh, my soul! but the milk is blue!)
She strayed and strayed and strayed and strayed
   (And I wail and I cry Wa-hoo!)

I've never seen her—nay, not I;
   (Oh, my soul! but the milk is blue!)
Yet were I that Cow I should want to die.
   (And I wail and I cry Wa-hoo!)
   But in vain my tears I strew.

Mr. A. Swinburne:

Only in dim, drowsy depths of a dream do I dare to delight in deliciously
      dreaming
Cows there may be of a passionate purple,—cows of a violent violet hue;

Ne'er have I seen such a sight, I am certain it is but a demi-delerious
      dreaming—
Ne'er may I happily harbour a hesitant hope in my heart that my dream may
      come true.

Sad is my soul, and my senses are sobbing so strong is my strenuous spirit to
  see one.
Dolefully, drearily doomed to despair as warily wearily watching I wait;

Thoughts thickly thronging are thrilling and throbbing; to *see* is a glorious
  gain—but to *be* one!
That were a darker and direfuller destiny, that were a fearfuller, frightfuller
  fate!

Carolyn Wells

Ernest Dowson (1867–1900)

Cynara Respondet*

So that's your fashion? What a coincidence:
I've been true in exactly the same sense.

Katherine McAlpine

*See Dowson's "*Non Sum Qualis Eram Bonae sub Regno Cynarae.*"

Edgar Lee Masters (1868–1950), et al.

from *Styx River Anthology**

The Blessed Damozel

I was one of those long, lanky, loose-jointed girls
Who fool people into believing
They are willowy and psychic and mysterious.
I was always hungry; I never ate enough to satisfy me,
For fear I'd get fat.
Oh, how little the world knows of the bitterness of life
To a woman who tries to keep thin!
Many thought I died of a broken heart,
But it was an empty stomach.
Then Mr. Rossetti wrote about me.
He described me all dolled up in some ladies' wearing apparel
That I wore at a fancy ball.
I had fasted all day, and had had my hair marcelled
And my face was corrected.
And I *was* a dream.
But he seemed to think he really saw me,
Seemed to think I appeared to him after my death.
Oh, fudge!
Those spiritualists are always seeing things!

Lucy

Yes, I am in my grave,
And you bet it makes a difference to him!
For we were to be married,—at least, I think we were,
And he'd made me promise to deed him the house.
But I had to go and get appendicitis,
And they took me to the hospital.

It was a nice hospital, clean,
And Tables Reserved For Ladies.
Well, my heart gave out.
He came and stood over my grave,
And registered deep concern.
And now, he's going around with that
Hen-minded Hetty What's-her-name!
Her with her Whistler's Mother and her Baby Stuart
On her best-room wall!
And I hate her, and I'm glad she squints.
Well, I suppose I've lived my life,
But it was Life in name only.
And I'm mad at the whole world!

Ophelia

No, it wasn't suicide,
But I had heard so much of those mud baths,
I thought I'd try one.
Ugh! it was a mess!
Weeds, slime, and tangled vines! Oh, me!
Had I been Annette Kellerman
Or even a real mermaid,
I had lived to tell the tale.
But I slid down and under,
And so Will Shaxpur told it for me.
Just as well.
But I think my death scene is unexcelled
By any in cold print.
It beats that scrawny, red-headed old thing of Tom Hood's
All hollow!

Annabel Lee

They may say all they like
About germs and micro-crocuses,—

Or whatever they are!
But my set opinion is,—
If you want to get a good, old-fashioned chills and fever,
Just poke around
In a damp, messy place by the sea,
Without rubbers on.
A good cold wind,
Blowing out of a cloud, by night,
Will give you a harder shaking ague
Than all the bacilli in the Basilica.
It did me.

Carolyn Wells

*Wells's sequence spoofs Masters's *Spoon River Anthology,* in which former residents of a Midwestern village speak their own epitaphs from beyond the grave.

Hilaire Belloc (1870–1953)

Variation on Belloc's "Fatigue"

I hardly ever tire of love or rhyme—
That's why I'm poor and have a rotten time.

Wendy Cope

Paul Laurence Dunbar (1872–1906)

For Paul Laurence Dunbar

Re: "Masks"

Some of us still wear the mask
that hides the smile:
payment of debt to human guile.

Grins concealed behind our so-called progress,
believing we have truly overcome
now that we go by way of front doors.

Jim Crow has flown the coop,
shooed out by Rosa Parks and others
of Montgomery, Alabama.

Though the crow's spirit continues
to nest atop trees holding leftover
wisps of rope attached to sturdy limbs
and the necks of Black men—
swaying reminders of the strange fruit
these trees bore.

We'll become sophisticated behind our masks,
no longer shuffling, beaming white-tooth grins,
happy darkies suppressing fury
with yessir, nosir, you sho' right boss,
holding on to quiet anger instead,
unable to halt the build-up of our silent rage
which began long before the proclamation
of emancipation in 1863.

And even after the marches, sit-ins,
foaming-mouth dogs biting black flesh,
swelled water hoses spewing hate,
LBJ's historical moments, his Johnny Hancock
guaranteeing civil rights for all Colored people
has not stopped the masquerade,
as we continue to let them see us
only while we wear the mask.

Linda Carter Brown

Twentieth–Century Poets

Robert Frost (1874–1963)

For Robert Frost

Easy as breath, without a trace of toil,
your lines uncoil, roll off the spool you wound
so that to shift one syllable would spoil
the spin of image or the flow of sound.
I turn your poem inside-out to see
what sleight-of-hand disguised as accident
transmutes the music into tapestry
without the knots and errors of intent,

but find your words are really only words
like those we use, and do not give away
the spell that works you into them. So birds
juggle their ordinary scales to say
extraordinary things. Like them, you came
to make our songs no longer quite the same.

Rhina P. Espaillat

Life-Binding

after "Range-Finding"

The bombing pressed a building pancake-stacked
And singed and blew soft blossoms off the trees
Like nothing known in cloudburst or in breeze.
The naked trees stood blackened, swiftly smoked.
Amidst all this a brown wasp flew and poked.
Some ants lay still beneath hills of hot debris.

Then one climbed through and others followed lead,
While on the sere concrete walk now there reeked
Fuel, gas leaks, tires melting on the street
And cables torn, like sinews, spewing sparks.
The sudden blowing car bomb tore the sky.
A wasp thought burning pollen fell from high,
But finding nothing sweet, transferred no spores.

Lenore Baeli Wang

Promises: On a Familiar Poem by Robert Frost*

What vows you made, I don't pretend to know,
Or how the snow seemed to your horse,
Or why you let him stand and shiver so.
You could have gone the self-same course
In spring. Where was it that you had to go?

Perhaps, if we were wise, we would suspect
That promises are fragile things,
Akin to snow's soft murmurings.
But I will woods-walk where you never stepped
And tell them how your promises were kept
Before the final sacrament—
A few, or more, or less, before you went;
A few, or most, or some, before you slept.

June Owens

*See Frost's "Stopping by Woods on a Snowy Evening."

Robert W. Service (1874–1958)

The Lady That's Known as Lou Gives R. W. Service
a Piece of Her Mind*

Our boys were whooping it up just fine till you swung through
our doors with your bank clerk's pad and swayback rhymes to make them
famous and put *me* down. Of course I'm pale through my rouge—

you'd look ghastly too if all winter you'd seen no sun, you'd curse
the slit of dusk at noon and no direct flights to Miami anytime soon.
As for your "literary success"—I confess I'll take ragtime over verse.

My bacon and beans banish *all* hungers. Your cholesterol
level may swerve but that's what I serve at the Malamute Saloon
when it's fifty below and radicchio refuses to grow at all.

As for Dangerous Dan, in bed he's a bust, and the golden dust
flecking his ebbing hair never panned out as a gold ring for me.
So when an old pal stumbles in fresh from the creek with a poke

and hits Haydn and Brahms in the gut—though he *is* a far ways
from Carnegie Hall over the frozen wastes with only our northern neons
for light, timber wolves howling off-key—and he *pays:* I shift my gaze.

Sure, I wish he'd washed, shaved his hairy face, and scrubbed the dirt
from his buckskin shirt, but you gotta melt a lotta snow and rub
a lotta skin and he'd been out in the cold so long he just wanted *in.*

Even so, both those blokes would rather hold their pokes of gold
than poke the hole in me. But nobody under the stars stole me from
    anyone—
I go where I please at whatever degrees, and baby, *I* run this bar.

You're stunned by that blizzard of bullets, shocked I'd kiss a corpse?
Well, t'hell with your so-wise lawyer guys. When the lights went out,
it was me (or I? what the heck), Two-Gun Mama just shuffling the deck.

Closing time! C'mon, honey, ditch those rhymes and climb my stairs.
Unhitch your starched collar, half-assed spats. See if you can service
me quicker than those poor stiffs. But before any amour, I gotta mop
     this bloody floor....

Elisavietta Ritchie

*See Service's "The Shooting of Dan McGrew."

Rainer Maria Rilke (1875–1926)

Answering to Rilke

Cramped by this indoor season—it's beginning
to feel as if winter will never go—
I chafe at my clutter of things, the flotsam gathered
around me like moss on a stone. "You must change
your life," says Rilke: and I say, Good;
let's start by simplifying, by tossing out.

Here's my wedding gown (when was I this thin?) out
of style, touched by mildew. A hard beginning!
Well, Rainer Maria, must I make good
on my vow to pry myself loose, let go,
"travel light," as the priesthood does, risk change?
Look how the sleeves are puffed, the waist gathered,

the neckline prim for our families gathered
to watch us spin a thread and send it out
into a common future. How people change
to braid into one, how such a beginning
dances into mystery! This must go
back into folded tissues, still mine, still good.

These are some books I meant to read a good
forty years ago. Still waiting, gathered
in dust, in silence. Each feels like a map. Go
find the girl who chose them? No, she's out
of print. But open one, smell: a beginning,
a beckoning route, that paper challenge to change.

Here, put them back: they salvage, safe from change,
read or unread, what was perhaps most good
in her, as she was at our beginning.
And look, my father's foreign coins, gathered

in lieu of travel: how toss them out?
Let them bear witness that he meant to go.

Old yellowed invitations: did I go?
Early pictures of people beyond change,
buried, estranged, divorced: childhood will out.
And in the requisite blue ribbon—Good
grief!—love letters long forgotten, gathered
to celebrate even a false beginning.

Nothing to go, Rilke. Maybe it's good
for change to surprise us in the moss we've gathered.
Figuring out that much is a beginning.

                                    Rhina P. Espaillat

Reason, My Dear Maria, Brings Us to Proximity

You've said, "I'm afraid, if my devils leave me,
my angels will take flight as well."
Very eloquent, one might almost say poetic.
But consider, Mr. Rilke, or may I call you Rainer
or do you prefer Maria?
We always prefer first names here. They distance us
from the real. I'd offer a glass of wine for our first
meeting. Do you have a drinking problem?
Though let me assure you it's not our job to judge
or condemn. Rather we try to investigate,
open you up to awareness of self,
take all that rich, opaque gray stew broiling around
beneath and give it specific, vivid, discernible color.
I love my work as I'm sure you can tell.
And I particularly love artists.
I consider myself an artist of a sort, taking the tied
psyche and artfully loosening the knot without whacking it off.

But enough of this implicit violence. Which reminds me—
have you given any thought to how you'll pay for treatment?
I understand you're a poet and though reasonably well-known,
this is Beverly Hills. So I hope you might have an angel
in the wings or a devil, if need be.
See my secretary on the way out; your 50 minutes are up.

Laurel Speer

John Masefield (1878–1967)

Light Lover*

Why don't you go back to the sea, my dear?
  I am not one who would hold you;
The sea is the woman you really love,
  So let hers be the arms that fold you.
Your bright blue eyes are a sailor's eyes,
  Your hungry heart is a sailor's too.
  And I know each port that you pass through
Will give one lass both bonny and wise
Who has learned light love from a sailor's eyes.
If you ever go back to the sea, my dear,
  I shall miss you—yes, can you doubt it?
But women have lived through worse than that,
  So why should we worry about it?
Take your restless heart to the restless sea,
  Your light, light love to a lighter lass,
  Who will smile when you come and smile when you pass.
Here you can only trouble me.
Oh, I think you had better go back to the sea!

Aline Kilmer

*See Masefield's "Sea-Fever."

Wallace Stevens (1879–1955)

A Word from Mrs. Wallace Stevens

Nothing grotesque or accidental as the day begins:
eggs-over-easy, buttered toast, black coffee before 7:00 a.m.,
The Hartford Courant, folded in three, by the breakfast plate.

I might be a painter myself: morning still life with poet.
He doesn't notice the yolks bleed cautiously, expertly
to the edge of frothy clouds, the way I've trained them.
He doesn't notice a pale hand sets peaches, pears, other fruit
in a bowl on the window sill.

Afternoons we're both busy: counting, sorting, mending.
I've never been to his office downtown,
but I know the way he leans forward over the ledger,
palm pressed sideways against the desk,
so his middle finger limps behind the pen as he
draws a number or crosses it out again—
one fine, thin black line—dead center.
He doesn't pause, look away from the stubborn columns to
consider the perfect brown mole
at the base of my throat.

In the evening, after boiled beef, a roast chicken,
he tells me taxes are going up again, or he's gotten a promotion.
Then he climbs the stairs, one-at-a-time, to the study:
there, vacation travels in similes to Naples, Havana, Bucks County, PA.
There, heroes and spectacles, blue music and botany,
the sun and moon and one, fine, plain pineapple.
There, the good chemistry of an orderly day, a baroque night.
He doesn't notice the torn corner of the heirloom pillow's been sewn.
He doesn't notice the sweet rusty stain where the thimble slipped
and an eager needle plucked the plump white flesh of my thumb.

Sima Rabinowitz

On Gari Melchers' Writing (1905) in the
Los Angeles County Museum

> The house was quiet and the world was calm.
> ——Wallace Stevens

How often did she make such quiet, one wonders,
This woman writing at a covered table—
Full summer light warming the roseate hues,
Mauve, red, and pink of dress and cloth and room.
A Wedgwood pier-glass shows three Roman figures
In ritual dance—cool neoclassic Graces—
Beside a clay pot of geraniums.
Her taste eclectic—like our modern lives—
Loving the past but settled in the living,

She seems meticulous—even, perhaps,
Like Edith Wharton, passionate for order,
Feeling, as she did, that in house and novel,
"Order, the beauty even of Beauty is."
Stevens, though you sought order in the sea
And grander heavens, the threat of nothingness
Unmanned you. Most women have no time for such,
For fate constrains them to immediate means,
The quiet art of keeping calm the house.

Helen Pinkerton

One Way of Looking at a Woman

> Among twenty snowy mountains,
> The only moving thing
> Was the eye of the blackbird.
> —"Thirteen Ways of Looking at a Blackbird"

There are thirteen ways of looking
at a blackbird,
there is one way of looking at a woman.

1

Among the late night stillnesses of city,
among its sleeping buildings,
the only moving thing I saw
was the eye of a woman.

2

I was of three minds,
like the night
in which there are two women.

3

The woman whirled in the midnight air.
It was a small part of the dance.

4

A man and a woman
are one. A woman and a woman
are one too.

5

I do not know which to prefer,
the kiss of a woman before,
or just after...

6

The shadow of a woman
left a kiss that could not be
understood by any.

7

O thin men of Manhattan
why do you imagine golden women?
Do you not see how the woman
walks around the feet
of the women about you?

8

I know
that a woman is involved
in what I know.

9

When the woman slipped from sight,
she marked the edge
of one of many breaths.

10

At the sight of women
dancing in a violet-silvery light,
even the thin men
would pause sharply.

11

I rode home in a taxi that evening.
For a moment a fear overtook me,
that I would not find my way back
to the eye of the woman.

12

The East River is moving.
A woman must be rising.

13

It was evening all afternoon,
it was raining,
and it was going to rain.
The woman stayed with me,
stayed very still, with me.

Phyllis Witte

William Carlos Williams (1883–1963)

This Is Just to Say*

(for William Carlos Williams)

I have just
asked you to
get out of my
apartment

even though
you never
thought
I would

Forgive me
you were
driving
me insane

Erica-Lynn Gambino

*See Williams's poem of the same title.

Enough

> So much depends / upon / a red wheel / barrow / glazed
> with rain / water / beside the white / chickens.
> —"The Red Wheelbarrow"

William Carlos Williams, I'm sick of your poem
about so much depending on a red wheelbarrow.

You have little idea just how much depends
on a once red wheelbarrow leaning against
a never-to-be-painted-again hen house.

So much depends on a mother forking human feces
from our privy into a precious wheelbarrow
and pushing the stench to the fields.

So much depends on a mother forking endless
stacks of chicken droppings into this wheelbarrow
and shoving it to the fields.

So much depends on a mother whose head brushes
the chicken roost, her hair crawling with lice
from those white magnolia chickens.

Stick to your antiseptic profession, Dr. Williams.

So much depends on a mother handling everyone's shit.
So much depends on a wheelbarrow, dumping her
into an early grave.

                                        Kathleen Iddings

The Profession*

an ode to William Carlos Williams

I

Exhausted of rhetoric
and anger
    I'm looking for poems.

Flowers in a desert
will not do,
    the rain is wrong,

it rains from a horrible bloom.
Music
    must grow immutable.

Doctors can do nothing
but reflect
    on broken glass,

sympathize but not correct,
their pain
    irreparable

loss they were born to,
take up
    instruments

instead of human
pursuit,
    wield

mirrors on their heads
look
    deep into the throat,

but it is the glass
that sees,
        wounded.

Never has the word
flower
        seemed more dried up,

sterile
as Venetian
        reproductions

mutations
made
        of fused sand.

II

Once there was thunder
and lightning,
        whirlwinds,

other voices,
prophecies,
        divination.

Men tore open the guts
of animals
        to find themselves,

but beginning
with the violation
        of lives—

thinking
to enlighten
        suffering,

our death,
in the bubbling blood
    of the slain;

christs,
our transmutations,
    crying

Eli, Eli, lama sabachthani,
that is to say
    who shall save them?

—we end
with the knives
    in ourselves.

Heal, heal, heal,
is the oath,
    like one to his dogs;

come under
control,
    that shadow of a rock.

Weep, weep rather
in Babylon
    beside the hanging gardens.

III

I am looking for poems.
Flowers change their strains
to the air, even stop
when they've gone too far,

though revived in glass houses,
or transplanted to blasts
in sand, salt water, or clouds.

To bind, holding, like a mirror,
faces together,
against rout, this time,

give rather, a bed
of daffodils, yellow pungent
as their snapped stems,

or even the greeney asphodel.
Such are the simples,
astringent as loving,
that only music immutable.

Judith Bishop

*Eli, Eli, lama sabachthani: "My God, my God, why hast thou forsaken me?" Christ's words on the Cross, *Matthew* 27:46.

Ezra Pound (1885–1972)

Astigmatism

> To Ezra Pound
> with much friendship and admiration and
> some differences of opinion

The Poet took his walking-stick
Of fine and polished ebony.
Set in the close-grained wood
Were quaint devices;
Patterns in ambers,
And in the clouded green of jades.
The top was of smooth, yellow ivory,
And a tassel of tarnished gold
Hung by a faded cord from a hole
Pierced in the hard wood,
Circled with silver.
For years the Poet had wrought upon this cane.
His wealth had gone to enrich it,
His experiences to pattern it,
His labour to fashion and burnish it.
To him it was perfect,
A work of art and a weapon,
A delight and a defence.
The Poet took his walking-stick
And walked abroad.

Peace be with you, Brother.

The Poet came to a meadow.
Sifted through the grass were daisies,
Open-mouthed, wondering, they gazed at the sun.
The Poet struck them with his cane.
The little heads flew off, and they lay

Dying, open-mouthed and wondering,
On the hard ground.
"They are useless. They are not roses," said the Poet.

Peace be with you, brother. Go your ways.

The Poet came to a stream.
Purple and blue flags waded in the water;
In among them hopped the speckled frogs;
The wind slid through them, rustling.
The Poet lifted his cane,
And the iris heads fell into the water.
They floated away, torn and drowning.
"Wretched flowers," said the Poet,
"They are not roses."

Peace be with you, Brother. It is your affair.

The Poet came to a garden.
Dahlias ripened against a wall.
Gillyflowers stood up bravely for all their short stature,
And a trumpet-vine covered an arbour
With the red and gold of its blossoms.
Red and gold like the brass notes of trumpets.
The Poet knocked off the stiff heads of the dahlias,
And his cane lopped the gillyflowers at the ground.
Then he severed the trumpet-blossoms from their stems.
Red and gold they lay scattered,
Red and gold, as on a battle field;
Red and gold, prone and dying.
"They were not roses," said the Poet.

Peace be with you, Brother.
But behind you is destruction, and waste places.

The Poet came home at evening,
And in the candle-light
He wiped and polished his cane.
The orange candle flame leaped in the yellow ambers,

And made the jades undulate like green pools.
It played along the bright ebony,
And glowed in the top of cream-coloured ivory.
But these things were dead,
Only the candle-light made them seem to move.
"It is a pity there were no roses," said the Poet.

Peace be with you, Brother. You have chosen your part.

Amy Lowell

Poem

> You are a poem, though
> your poem's naught.
> —Pound to H.D.

   I have a beard, smeared
with sweet traces of bees,
       the source of my verse.

   I am a fountain
in desert wilderness
       welling from mountains.

   some god has visited
with flame, a valley ripe
       with Canaan's promises,

   my glad gates flung wide.
Enter and I will sing.
       I am harp and lyre

   and love song, spilling
from these glazed lips the taste
       of some golden thing.

Carol E. Miller

Robinson Jeffers (1887–1962)

Una Jeffers to Her Husband, Robinson

All those rocks piled up
by your hard hands
to make our Tor House home.

All that frowning stone
surrounded by slender picket fence—
perfect metaphor for you:
romance protecting rock,
rock hiding honey in its core.

Town-folk crossed the street,
believing you as harsh as your philosophy.
But your twin sons knew better.
I knew better.
I was there when you buried the dog
beneath our bedroom window.
I carry your love poems in my marrow.

I agree man loves himself too much
and raises himself above the stars.
I agree hawks are as admirable as men,
oceans unfathomable and unmindful
of the fragile freight
upon the briny, brilliant blue.

While standing next to you at continent's end,
I see wind-twisted trees,
understand with you that
greater forces rule us than ourselves.

But my dear—
I also see chinks beneath your flint,

man/father/lover/anguished poet
who loves not man apart
but everything in its entirety.
And then your inhumanness
becomes superbly human.

Barbara Brent Brower

T.S. Eliot (1888–1965)

Waste Land Limericks

I

In April one seldom feels cheerful;
Dry stones, sun and dust make me fearful;
Clairvoyantes distress me,
Commuters depress me—
Met Stetson and gave him an earful.

II

She sat on a mighty fine chair,
Sparks flew as she tidied her hair;
She asks many questions,
I make few suggestions—
Bad as Albert and Lil—what a pair!

III

The Thames runs, bones rattle, rats creep;
Tiresias fancies a peep—
A typist is laid,
A record is played—
Wei la la. After this it gets deep.

IV

A Phoenician called Phlebas forgot
About birds and his business—the lot,

Which is no surprise,
Since he'd met his demise
And been left in the ocean to rot.

V

No water. Dry rocks and dry throats,
Then thunder, a shower of quotes
From the Sanskrit and Dante.
Da Damyata. Shantih.
I hope you'll make sense of the notes.

Wendy Cope

Mermaid's Song*

I'm one of the mermaids in Prufrock's Song;
I'm his temptation, deliciously wrong.

He longs for excitement and strife
(Remember the drum and the fife?)
But he stays with his dull wife,
His dull life,
Like a dull knife.

I grow young, I grow young,
I become the fish I swim among!

Am I a Lesbian? Not quite,
Though I love women;
It's just that no man dares
To brave the waters that I swim in—
They admire the way I play the lyre,
But blame me for my beauty;

They send me secret gifts
       but will not visit,
They're so absorbed by Duty.

In the room men come
Like Tweedledee and Tweedledum,
Dreading to be in the minority,
Talking about the Transit Authority.

My breast is bare
(Life is too short for secrets);
I decline to sit in a chair.

But I'm tired of being told how strong I am:
What rot, I'm not
Any stronger than any other creature,
In fact, I have a handicap—this tail—
Or hadn't you noticed my nether feature?
Actually, I happen to be quite frail,
Have to take frequent naps.
The difference between us
Is that I've made choices
Because I had no choice
But to make choices,
And when I heard voices,
I said, "Well, perhaps."

I sing, I sing, so as not to be grim;
I thrash about, so give me room;
I also cry a lot;
It is my doom
To be courted by Prufrocks
Who cannot, will not, swim.

Verna Safran

*See "The Love Song of J. Alfred Prufrock."

A Small Quarrel with T.S. Eliot

> Every phrase and every sentence is an end and a beginning.
> —*Little Gidding*, V; line 11

If love is not the best of poems ever penned,
Why does all language dwindle down to a single yes
And every kiss is our beginning and our end?

Before affection's nameless fires, the book will bend,
All power of prose, each written line will acquiesce.
If love is not the best of poems ever penned,

Then I am neither literate nor comprehend
What love has written on our bones when we caress
And every kiss is our beginning and our end.

Silk speech of eyes, the happiness of hands transcend
Mere talk of tongue; the printed page lies passionless
If love is not the best of poems ever penned.

What added depth to intimacy do letters lend
When we become two Roman candles, incandesce,
And every kiss is our beginning and our end?

If bounden to believe what sentences pretend,
We read in runics as we silently undress;
If love is not the best of poems ever penned,
Still, every kiss is our beginning and our end.

June Owens

e.e. cummings (1894–1962)

The Boys I *Mean**

The boys *I* mean are too refined.
They get their way with just a smile.
They never twitch or fall apart.
They like to make you wait a while.

The boys *I* mean have charcoal eyes
and long-lashed glances as they watch.
Their frayed black coats graze scuffed-up shoes.
Their tar-burned tongues tell only lies.

The boys I love have silly pasts
that stay away like beaten wives.
Their alphabets are M and E.
They mix their drinks with hunting knives.

The girls they love look just like me
and wear barbed tongues like cellophane.
They smoke whatever comes their way.
They fuck for pleasure and for pain.

The boys *I* mean have too much grace
and too much money, luck and brains.
They crash their cars with little haste.
They like to park in fire lanes.

The boys *I* mean can talk all night,
and even then they still don't care.
They pose and posture, preen and pout.
They always have such pretty hair.

The boys I love will break your heart
with granite fists and brooding stares.

They'll fuck you anywhere you want,
in alleys, cars or hallway stairs.

They say whatever's on your mind.
They cannot, will not, do not dance.
The boys *I* mean are too refined.
They shake your world with just a glance.

Julia Goldberg

*See Cummings's "The Boys I Mean."

Robert Graves (1895–1985)

Pantoum to a Bearded Muse on Lines by Robert Graves

"A Muse does not wear whiskers."
Then shave my dear or bear the fate:
Disqualified by facial hair.
My poems will languish while I wait.

Then shave my dear or bear the fate
prescribed for us by Robert Graves.
My poems will languish while I wait.
I'll pass the time with rants and raves

prescribed for us by Robert Graves .
"It is dangerous to fight the Muse."
I'll pass the time with rants and raves,
indecent rhymes, the Zoo Bar blues.

"It is dangerous to fight the Muse."
Would I fight you, my bearded one?
Indecent rhymes, the Zoo Bar blues
bring back your inspiration.

Would I fight you, my bearded one?
Without your touch, I cannot write.
Bring back your inspiration;
push these lines to Helicon's height.

Without your touch I cannot write.
Your metaphorical fingers can
push these lines to Helicon's height.
Why cannot the Muse be a man?

Your metaphorical fingers can
tease and warm my frigid verse.

Why cannot the Muse be a man?
I call upon You to negate this curse.

Tease and warm my frigid verse.
Let Robert Graves spin where he lies.
I call upon You to negate this curse.
(He'll never be Muse in anyone's eyes.)

Let Robert Graves spin where he lies.
Disqualified by facial hair,
he'll never be Muse in anyone's eyes.
"A Muse does not wear whiskers."

Kathleene West

The Muse Says She's Finished

for Robert Graves

Says she's turning off
the magic spring.
She no longer needs
their faces hovering
about her to feel useful.
No longer wants their mouths
breaking her calm,
poisoning her revery
with the rank breath
of their desire.

Says she's putting down
her trowel. No more
dropping a perfect
berry in their mouths
while they are snoring.

Did they think such
succulence grew wild,
that she hadn't toiled,
stirred amendments into
rocky soil for centuries
to yield one tart image?

She supposes it's her own
fault—biting at the first
tug on her line, offering
herself without a struggle,
letting them grab her
by the tail and pose.
How many times did they
suppose she'd let her
spine be sliced away,
her flesh devoured
without a blessing?

Judith Sornberger

Sir John Betjeman (1906–1984)

Modern Middlesex*

Elaine replies to Sir John

Thank God, nearing Ruislip Gardens.
Then I'll leave this wretched train
And that man who's begging pardons
As he ogles me again,
Eyes my jacket (not quite Jaeger).
He looks vicar-like, but vaguer,
Branding me by brand-name fashion
In his comfy, cosy passion,
Fantasising of suspenders in a modest county lane.

I'm far from the sort he's after—
Jolly girls with mummy's flair,
English rippling muscled laughter—
They just make me tear my hair.
I've got budgets in my brief-case,
Contracts, long-term plans, no leave-space,
Spread-sheets (lap-top based), reports,
Regional Directors' thoughts:
I can't pander to your fancies—horsy girls and good fresh air.

Dear Sir John, the times are changing.
Women: street-wise, tough, urbane,
Running companies, arranging
World-wide deals from Minsk to Maine.
Tea-shops, tennis, county dances,
Whispered words and covert glances—
Gone. We function now on e-mail:
That's the modern, working female.
Now my mobile phone is ringing—please excuse me. Hello? Spain?

D.A. Prince

*See Betjeman's "Middlesex."

W.H. Auden (1907–1973)

*At Auden's Museum**

About everything, in fact, they were wrong,
the Old Masters. Nothing is happening,
then—except them, the Old Masters. They are happening

when they see someone falling and someone else not
falling, framed by them with a costly ship,
or game, or horse's ass. When they see everyone

falling, in anyone falling, then they are not
Masters anymore—but men, who repent
their mastery, want to forswear it,

but can't. Unmastered, they paint master
work: they take suffering and make it
dangle, broken-winged, treed, becalmed.

Stephanie Strickland

*See Auden's "Musèe des Beaux Arts."

Public Journal

VERSES INSPIRED BY A DAY SPENT IN
COMMUNION WITH THE BRIGHT YOUNG
MEN OF ENGLISH VERSE

Christopher Isherwood, Stephen Spender,
   Auden and L. MacNeice—
I can't come along on an all-night bender,
   But I'll have a quick one with you.

It is four in the afternoon. Time still for a poem,
A poem not topical, wholly, or romantic, or metaphysic,
But fetched from the grab-bag of my mind and gaudy with
Symbol, slogan, quotation, and even music.
And many a Marxian maxim and many allusions
To a daft system and a world-disorder.
I will mention machines and the eight-hour day and
Czechoslovakia and the invaded border.

I will speak of love and I will do it slyly,
Unloosing the sacred girdle with a tired air,
Taking particular pains to notice the elastic garters
And the literal underwear.

I will put learning into my poem, for I acquired learning
At Cambridge or Oxford, it does not matter which.
But I'll freshen it up with slang which I got by ear,
Though it may sound a little off pitch.
And I'll be casual with rhymes for that is the trend,
Fashionable as the black hat of Anthony Eden.
I may put them at the middle of the stanza instead of the end,
For really amazing effect.
Or perhaps I'll find that assonance heightens the meaning better.
Yes, definitely, I prefer the latter.

Well, it will be sport, writing my private hates
And my personal credo.
I must bring in how I went to Spain on a holiday,

And how cold it was in Toledo.
There was a bootblack, too, in Madrid,
Who gave my shoes a burnish.
He told me something important which I cannot repeat,
For although I understand Spain, I do not understand Spanish.

I will put tarts in my poem, and tenement people,
The poor but not the meek;
And pieces of popular songs for a hint of nostalgia,
And bits of Greek.
I shall be tough and ardent and angry-eyed,
Aware that the world is dying, gasping, its face grown pallid;
But quick to embalm it in language as an aspic
Enfolds the chicken salad.

Now it is five o'clock. The poem is finished
Like Poland, like the upper classes, like Sunday's roast.
I must straighten my waistcoat and see that it goes straight out
By the evening post.

For what is left for us? Only
The stanza a day,
And the American royalties, and an inherited income,
To keep the wolf at bay.

Phyllis McGinley

Czeslaw Milosz (b. 1911)

Reading, Dreaming, Hiding

> You asked me what is the good of reading the Gospels in Greek.
> —Milosz, "Readings"

You were reading. I was dreaming
The color blue. The wind was hiding
In the trees and rain was streaming
Down the windows, full of darkness.

Rain was dreaming in the trees. You
Were full of darkness. The wind was streaming
Down the window, the color blue.
I was reading and hiding.

The wind was full of darkness and rain
Was streaming in the trees and down the window.
The color blue was full of darkness, dreaming
In the wind and trees. I was reading you.

Kelly Cherry

Karl Shapiro (b. 1913)

The Art of Nature

> This is the nature of art, that it is
> wholly and immediately apprehended,
> like a tree or a woman.
> —Karl Shapiro

Consider birches on their knees,
bowed, now, and silvered who were once
girlish, their lithe limbs shivering,
their bright, wet heads thrown to the sun.

Consider the laurel, her crown
of stooped crows, so many clinging
pairs of common claws, so little
praise in their harsh throats, hawking.

Consider these when you look up
expecting a calm horizon:
familiar trees flocked with familiar birds
will be walking, almost human.

Carol E. Miller

John Berryman (1914–1972)

a poem with capital letters

john berryman asked me to write a poem about roosters.
elizabeth bishop, he said, once wrote a poem about roosters.
do your poems use capital letters? he asked. *like god?*
i said. *god no,* he said, *like princeton!* i said,
god preserve me if i ever write a poem about princeton, and i thought,
o john berryman, what has brought me into this company of poets
where the masculine thing to do is use capital letters
and even princeton struts like one of god's betters?

Jane Cooper

Reply to a Dream Song*

> Them lady poets must not marry, pal.

Maybe them macho poets should not marry, man.
What woman with half a brain would care to be
cooped up for life with the likes of Mr. Berryman,
or Dylan, stewed before it's time for tea?
Roethke?—fancy a midnight romp with him
in the greenhouse! Fancy a fling with crazy Pound
or Lowell, in and out of the loony bin.
Why, with so many sensible men around—
solvent, attractive, sober—would I choose
poor messed-up Delmore? Give a girl a breather!
Who'd want to slaughter sheep with old Ted Hughes?
Far as that goes, I wouldn't swoon much, either,
for Auden, Crane or Uncle Walt (but they
weren't all that keen on women, anyway).

Katherine McAlpine

*See Berryman's Dream Song #187, of which Joyce Carol Oates has written: "Centuries of women poets are dismissed in a drunk's baby prattle, and those who are considered worthy of special attention are nonetheless 'lady poets' the (male) poet would not want to 'bed.' (And would the objects of Berryman's boozy sexual interest want to 'bed' him? A question the poet seems not to consider.)"

Weldon Kees (1914–1955?)

Note from the Imaginary Daughter*

I have no daughter, I desire none.

Mother always swore your plunge was faked
so you could vanish—unknown—into travel.
I waited for a postcard—some sign I could take
as proof she was right. Some thread I'd unravel
back to you—wherever you were. Mexico,
she guessed.
                          In pictures you look sad but kind.
Mother said you were brilliant but confused.
She said I might not like the man I'd find—
if I ever did.
                          She said you'd only used
her love for art; still she wished you'd let her go
along.
                          She kept the poems. The paintings, too.
And I composed myself a father who
filled my desire—a man too real to mourn.
Some nights I dream you dead. Some days, unborn.

Grace Bauer

*See Kees's "For My Daughter." The poet disappeared mysteriously in 1955.

Dylan Thomas (1914–1953)

Dylan, We Were Like Those Flimsy Moons*

Two moons there are, one laked, one skied,
As big as tops of kettledrums,
As bright as brasswork pendulums.
Diaphanous. Dissatisfied.
They languish on the lips of night
But, finding meager comfort there,
They hold each other with a stare
As primitive as candlelight.

Love, we were like those flimsy moons
That look into each other's shine,
Perhaps to hear if riddle runes
Still singing there will tell why either's
Incandescence dimmed, which blame was mine,
Which imperfections yours, which neither's.

June Owens

*The speaker of this and the following two poems is Thomas's wife, Caitlin, with whom he had an intense, symbiotic, and often mutually self-destructive relationship.

Caitlin to Dylan: In Memoriam*

The force that through the green fuse drives the flower
Drove you to drink? That has been said—
And I your destroyer!
And I am dumb to tell you, crooked rose,
My youth was bent by the same wintry fever.

The lips of time leeched to the fountain head;
Love dripped and gathered, but the fallen blood
Calmed not my sores.
And I am dumb to tell our love's tomb
How at my sheet went the same crooked worm.

Margaret Rogers

*See Thomas's "The Force That through the Green Fuse Drives the Flower."

Doubting Thomas

Mopping up his ordinary puke,
       himself a quarreling sea,
Listening to genius
       dwindle into gibberish,
Watching him wow them
       with candles on the stage,
Knowing he's fast extinguishing
       his own—

If he was what Eliot called
       "a minor poet,"
Would I have put out and put up
       with the shame of it,
Or would I have gone ungentle
       into that good night,
And would mothers be naming their daughters
       Caitlin after me?

We overlook so much
When deft those dragon words
       pluck our secret lyre.

Verna Safran

Bodies You Broke

(after Dylan Thomas, "This Bread I Break")

Oats we've rolled and bread you broke,
you break it still, now watch us rise
up, back in time, and plunge your heads
through crusts you've cracked
deep in dough we'll roll with bones.

Once you bled us summer nights,
tearing flesh when flesh was tight.
You kneaded hearts to sow
wild oats. The crusts that formed
you pulled apart. But now we steam.

You milked our flesh and vined our hearts
till veins ran dry—
thorns shook loose and skin grew crusts,
our hearts grew thick; just try to drink
or bite us now, your teeth will crack.

Lenore Baeli Wang

Charles Causley (b. 1917)

My Friend Melissa*

after Charles Causley

My friend Melissa, eighteen,
  Smokes like a chimney,
Ran into trouble two years back
  With the local gentry.

Pastor and mayor's sons
  Climbed atop her.
The psychologist took one look at Melissa.
  Fixed her proper.

Talked of the crime of youth,
  The innocent victim.
Melissa never said a kind word
  To contradict him.

Melissa of French Street,
  Back of the City Mission,
Daughter of a crack pusher,
  Blamed television.

Psychotherapy triumphed.
  Everyone felt fine.
Things went deader.
  Melissa reeled in her line.

Melissa lost a thing or two
  Changing orientation.
First skirt, second innocence,
  The old irresolution.

Found herself a girl-friend,
  Sharp hair, drab colors.
Melissa drives a Volvo,
  Sued for one million dollars.

College boys on the corner
  Polish their black Blazers,
Look at old Melissa,
  Eyes like dull razors.

"I don't need hassle," says Melissa.
  "My partner's a fox.
What you're not, she's got, fellers.
  You can keep your mean cocks."

Pastor got a TV show,
  Mayor, in the end the same.
The psychologist incorporated.
  "Life," said Melissa, "'s a game."

Consider then the case of Melissa,
  College boys, pastor, mayor, shrink.
Who was the victor and who was the victim?
  Think.

Nola Garrett

*See Causley's "My Friend Maloney."

Robert Lowell (1917–1977)

A Muse of Water*

We who must act as handmaidens
To our own goddess, turn too fast,
Trip on our hems, to glimpse the muse
Gliding below her lake or sea,
Are left, long-staring after her,
Narcissists by necessity;

Or water-carriers of our young
Till waters burst, and white streams flow
Artesian, from the lifted breast:
Cup-bearers then, to tiny gods,
Imperious table-pounders, who
Are final arbiters of thirst.

Fasten the blouse, and mount the steps
From kitchen taps to Royal Barge,
Assume the trident, don the crown,
Command the Water Music now
That men bestow on Virgin Queens;
Or, goddessing above the waist,

Appear as swan on Thames or Charles
Where iridescent foam conceals
The paddle-stroke beneath the glide:
Immortal feathers preened in poems!
Not our true, intimate nature, stained
By labor, and the casual tide.

Masters of civilization, you
Who moved to river bank from cave,
Putting up tents, and deities,

Though every rivulet wander through
The final, unpolluted glades
To cinder-bank and culvert-lip,

And all the pretty chatterers
Still round the pebbles as they pass
Lightly over their watercourse,
And even the calm rivers flow,
We have, while springs and skies renew,
Dry wells, dead seas, and lingering drouth.

Water itself is not enough.
Harness her turbulence to work
For man: fill his reflecting pools.
Drained for his cofferdams, or stored
In resevoirs for his personal use:
Turn switches! Let the fountains play!

And yet these buccaneers still kneel
Trembling at the water's verge:
"Cool River-Goddess, sweet ravine,
Spirit of pool and shade, inspire!"
So he needs poultice for his flesh.
So he needs water for his fire.

We rose in mists and died in clouds
Or sank below the trammeled soil
To silent conduits underground,
Joining the blind-fish, and the mole.
A gleam of silver in the shale:
Lost murmur! Subterranean moan!

So flows in dark caves, dries away,
What would have brimmed from bank to bank,
Kissing the fields you turned to stone,
Under the boughs your axes broke.
And you blame streams for thinning out,
Plundered by man's insatiate want?

Rejoice when a faint music rises
Out of a brackish clump of weeds,
Out of the marsh at ocean-side,
Out of the oil-stained river's gleam,
By the long causeways and gray piers
Your civilizing lusts have made.

Discover the deserted beach
Where ghosts of curlews safely wade:
Here the warm shallows lave your feet
Like tawny hair of magdalens.
Here, if you care, and lie full-length,
Is water deep enough to drown.

Carolyn Kizer

*Author's note: "'A Muse of Water' was written in direct response to Lowell, who in Theodore Roethke's kitchen, remarked that the Germans had it right in saying that women should stick to church, children, and kitchen. So I rushed home and wrote this poem, which in early drafts had several references to Lowell. When I thought it over, I decided that Lowell didn't deserve the poem and took out all references to him. However, I overlooked the Charles River, which hangs in there like a vermiform appendix."

*What I Heard**

You have bid me speak,
and so I shall,
though not with anything
resembling "flaming insight,"
only my own voice:

Whose faults were they,
Robert, that one bed,
that apartness of bodies,

and desire lost, that knowing
we could not come back as gulls?

You never asked, but, yes,
I grieved for the Maine house;
I've let its hill and birds
stay round, flying in my memory,
crowded for something worth holding onto.

Wish them well if you must,
those interloping pretenders
to what we knew (so briefly
knew) of love, its little dark
attachments, its many-ghosted deaths.

In our talk-night breath
and in the creak of our hearts,
I heard a world of endings, Robert,
more than mere snowplows on hills.
Oh, you'd be surprised what I heard.

June Owens

---

*See Lowell's "My Old Flame," addressed to the poet's first wife, novelist Jean Stafford.

Charles Bukowski (1920–1994)

The Muse Interrupts My Rant at Charles Bukowski
over His Popularity among Otherwise Fine Young Men

The Muse is a fine old broad. She can forgive
your low opinion of women and most men,
but maybe not the way you chose to live,
puking your guts on her gifts again and again.

Your low opinion of women and most men
suggests that you weren't too crazy about yourself,
puking your guts on her gifts again and again,
then pulling another bottle or book from the shelf.

Suggest that you weren't too crazy about yourself.
See if I care. The gift is given to pass.
Pulling your bottle, your books off of the shelf,
these kids think a real poet has to be drunk on his ass. . .

"See.
        If I care, the gift is given. To pass
the loutish would limit poetry to the pure.
These kids think a real poet's got to be drunk? On his ass
my colleague included the drunks and the whores on his tour."

The loutish would limit poetry to the pure.
(But maybe not the way you chose.) To live,
my colleague included the drunks and the whores on his tour.
The Muse is a fine old broad. She can forgive.

Susan Blackwell Ramsey

Paul Celan (1920–1970)

*Three-Part Invention for Celan**

I

Put out two teacups:
one for Amherst,
one for Ukraine.

Fill each snowy hollow
with all the wasted
words. I know the kittens
are starving, and it's
really something how those trees
have lasted until their high
architecture sings.

I also know—haven't you
always told me?—that
time detonates its flowers
in icy hollows beyond
the lofty trees so that
yonder deaf child might
cradle his assault weapon
and the old volunteer
can keep on pistol-whipping
the yews until their tears thaw.

I know that hunched child
has never wept. He aims
guerilla couplets into
the answering machine.

This, too, you predicted, along
with ice crystals

in bleached sockets
at each place setting:
pistol there, assault weapon here.

In Amherst the old volunteer
has no song for us.
In Ukraine the stone-hearted
child has no place at
any table and the snowy
hollows ring out welcome.

II

On February's first day
a young oak holds onto
her wind-torn wrapper.

Or is it an old tart,
bagged limbs, bones
rattling down, down to
the subterranean trains?
How mercilessly aimed!
They bore networked entrails
through a treeless underground
of root-cut hollows.

The beaten young oak.
The bagged bones.

III

Approach empty fields,
keeping your friendly
distance.

You are riding bareback,
gripping white mane.

Sing. Gust. Aim
death-saving secrets
unto everlasting.

On no track else
has the scent of violets
been this potent.

Patricia Wilcox

*Celan, a Holocaust survivor who lost both parents to the death camps, left what many consider the finest poetic testimony to the dark legacy of World War II. He lived after the war in Paris; his poetry, written in German, was influenced by the French Surrealists, and he was also an admirer and translator of Emily Dickinson. Wilcox's poem echoes Celan's surrealistic imagery and syntactic idiosyncracies.

Richard Wilbur (b. 1921)

Aubade on Troost Avenue*

Hommage to Richard Wilbur

The eyes open to a Hopper painting.
It is the Thriftway Cleaners at six in the morning,
hanging for a moment in a hushed gallery
of gray rain. Inside the yellow window
a woman in an orange uniform attends an army

in plastic bags, limp on its hangers,
empty of arms and legs. Back of the counter,
there are the clothes waiting for the daily orders
of fresh feeling, filling whoever will wear them
with the dignity of their crisp dry-cleaning.

Now they are marching in circles as the woman
flips the switch for inspection. Suddenly stopping,
they sway towards her as she slouches to the door,
yawns, stretches, clicks the lock, and turns
the red placard from CLOSED to OPEN,

opening so the world can come in and regain
with barely a word, its clothing and its colors.
Oh, let there be nothing today but cleaning,
nothing but warm vapor and the steamy chemical
smell of linen and wool pleated and creased.

Let them emerge from their rank confinement,
these suits and dresses and coats for the well-to-do;
let heroes go forth in the latest fashion
of fine attitudes, while the sleepy attendant
loads and reloads her machine.

Barbara Loots

*See Wilbur's "Love Calls Us to the Things of This World."

Philip Larkin (1922–1985)

My Night with Philip Larkin*

Rendezvous with dweeby Philip in the shower:
"Aubade" taped up on pale blue tile;
I can hear him grumbling through the falling water.
Uncurling steam is scented with a trace of bile.
And I'm as grateful as a thankless child can be.
Someone has been here in this night with me,
Someone whose bitterness, I want to say,
Is even more impressive than my own.
Talking with Larkin on the great white telephone
I let the night be washed out into day

Until it's safe enough to go lie down
And dream of my librarian, my bride.
Perhaps he sits and watches in his dressing gown;
I know he won't be coming to my side
For fumblings and words he simply can't get out.
That stuff was never what it was about
When he would wake at four o'clock to piss
And part the curtains, let the moon go on
With all the things worth doing, and not done,
The things that others do instead of this.

Rachel Loden

*See Larkin's "Aubade" and "Sad Steps."

Alan Dugan (b. 1923)

The Red-Haired Waitress*

I used to smile with more than teeth.
Sometimes at night I dream these teeth huge,
biting into the hands I feed.
A smile, they tell me, makes the difference
between a clink and a rustle
in the tip jar. So I pull my lips back,
back from these not-so-whites,
remembering what I saw once on cable tv:
how monkeys and dogs grin to threaten,
naked teeth a flashed warning,
a do-not-disturb sign drawing itself with blood.
Watch me smile, friend, and open your wallet.
Here's a threat you don't even know about.

Kel Munger

*See Dugan's "To a Red-Headed Do-Good Waitress."

Donald Justice (b. 1925)

Women at Forty

> Men at forty
> learn to close softly
> the doors to rooms they will
> not be coming back to.
>   —Donald Justice, "Men at Forty"

Women at forty
have learned to open
the doors
of our estrangement.
We enter possession
of rooms and worlds
that we have held
in trust.

At forty we
stand firmly before
the frankness of mirrors,
face a lover's eyes
more proud
in daylight
than we ever were
at twenty. As lovers
our arms are strong,
from sweeping away
a lifetime
of imperfections.

To women at forty
perfection is a burden.
The wild thread

in the cloth,
the splattering of glaze
write their own distinctive names.
At forty we embrace
our differences
as we do returning children,
spin acceptance
around them
like tangled kitestrings,
nests of fishline,
hairs that marry in a brush.

Women at forty
savor the past.
We whet our lips
with wisdom.
Gone is the smile
of youth, flashing
like a searchlight.
The smile at forty slips
within. We take pleasure
in ourselves
for a change.

If women at forty are silent,
it is the quiet of winter
waiting knowingly
for spring. We cultivate
our growth, make the most
of fertile ground.
At forty we
are winds from where we please,
outfitters of our own journeys.
Where there is no road,
we believe one.

At forty we
are born-again believers,

beginners, and takers of risks.
We cast our bread
upon the waters
for the sheer joy
of the exercise,
raising no hope
of a miraculous return.

Kathleen M. Bogan

Robert Bly (b. 1926)

Walking through a Cornfield in the Middle of Winter, I Stumble over a Cow Pie and Think of the Sixties Press

Blue toads are dying all over Minnesota
among the cantaloupes, the ripening waists
of the banana republics.

The horses brush flies with their tails.
The flies are Literary Establishment flies,
Trujillo flies, Franco flies, General Motors flies.
The horses love each other
but do not know what to do about it.
They nuzzle the fence posts affectionately.
The fence posts grow larger and fill up the whole horizon
in a sea of turning eagles.

I shall print my friends on a Thursday, in Paris,
in the rain, from an untouchable cave
behind my Guggenheim.
And watch the Wops scribble all over the statues
behind the Villa d'Este.

All the Shell stations are bathed in a luminous film
iridescent with gas.

It is also good to be poor, and live in the hen house
with the droppings of last year's chickens
blazing into magazines under my feet.

Barbara Harr

Allen Ginsberg (1926–1997)

Bowling Green, Sewing Machine! *

Along the street and under the stars,
I'm making my way to the 7–11.
Solano Avenue seems suddenly endless.
I have a lot on my mind.

I'm in love. With you, Allen Ginsberg.
And I couldn't care less!
So, you are gay; I am straight.
We're both poets.

Oh, Allen, you must listen.
You've no idea. We have so much in common.
You love sunflowers; I love sunflowers, too.
I know where they grow like natural Van Gogh
Along the winding streets of Berkeley.

There are so many secret gardens!
And now the moon blooms—almost full.

Come on, Allen. Won't you, please, play your harmonium.
Such music goes perfect with jasmine perfume.
Mantras linger in the air…
Om…I'm remembering:
1968; NYU; You're on the stage; How you sing!
Songs of Innocence and Experience.
I'm one among the audience.
Your wild-man hairs are corkscrewing around,
Exposing your loneliest fathers' traditions.

My own long hair keeps pulling me forward....
Look up. We're under the BART overpass.

And now, let's sit down. There's no law against it.
There's something I need to discuss.
I take it for granted no subject's off-limits;
No pride can come between us.

Come on. Sit closer. Face to face.
Let me look deep into your four-eyes through mine.
If we wore lenses ground by Spinoza,
What are the odds? Would we be smarter?

So you are a Buddhist; I'm only me.
We are that we are. We both are.

Sometimes I can find no way out.
I feel trapped inside my own skin.
I wander lost in my tiny apartment;
Believe me, it's not—labyrinthian.

It's more like the closet
Young Jesus said
We should do our praying in.

My one prayer. My only prayer.
That all my failures are worth all their trying.

But tonight is young and the Häagen-Dazs beckons!

In and out of the 7–11...It's so easy...I float...
Where are you? Oh, Allen! Why do you disappear?
I must walk home now
Soliloquizing
Under this summer solstice moon.

So what if it's true everything is connected!

So what if it's true everything counts!
Quick. Look. Lick my fingers.
This pint of coffee ice cream
melts.

Peggy Landsman

*Author's note: "'Bowling Green, Sewing Machine' is the song sung by Sidney Poitier in the 1958 film, *The Defiant Ones*. Only my muse can tell us why it is also the title of my poem." See Ginsberg's "A Supermarket in California," in which the poet has a vision of Walt Whitman.

W.D. Snodgrass (b. 1926)

*To a Friend Whose Work Has Come to Triumph**

Consider Icarus, pasting those sticky wings on,
testing that strange little tug at his shoulder blade,
and think of that first flawless moment over the lawn
of the labyrinth. Think of the difference it made!
There below are the trees, as awkward as camels;
and here are the shocked starlings pumping past
and think of innocent Icarus who is doing quite well:
larger than a sail, over the fog and the blast
of the plushy ocean, he goes. Admire his wings!
Feel the fire at his neck and see how casually
he glances up and is caught, wondrously tunneling
into that hot eye. Who cares that he fell back to the sea?
See him acclaiming the sun and come plunging down
while his sensible daddy goes straight into town.

Anne Sexton

*According to Sexton's biographer, Diane Wood Middlebrook, Sexton wrote this poem for Snodgrass upon his winning the Pulitzer Prize in 1960.

John Ashbery (b. 1927)

*I Scream in America**

With few, if any, apologies to John Ashbery

It's as if ink has taken on
a death of its own
the old pictures won't fall clean
stick awkwardly in the craw
on their way off the canvas

Nothing's downstream but fish
no worry they can't swim
they're dead after all
all that's left to do is complain

Forgetting we come here
in a crowd, proudly, on purpose,
rudely applauding
the sad decay of something.

Fill your poems with careful
nonsense packaged prettily
in ribbons of language

Diane Engle

*See Ashbery's "Ice Cream in America."

James Wright (1927-1980)

Elevens

There is one story and one story only
—Robert Graves, "To Juan at the Winter Solstice"

James A. Wright, my difficult older brother,
I'm in an airplane over your Ohio.
Twice a week, there and back, I make this journey
to Cincinnati.

You are six books I own and two I borrowed.
I'm the songs about the drunk on the runway
and leaving your lover for the airport, first
thing in the morning.

You were fifty-two when you died of cancer
of the tongue, apologist for the lonely
girls who were happened to near some bleak water.
Tell me about it.

When my father died young, my mother lost it.
I am only three years younger than he was.
The older brother and the younger brother
that I never had

died young, in foreign cities, uncomforted.
Does anybody not die uncomforted?
My friend Sonny had her lovers around her
and she died also.

Half drunk on sunlight in my second country,
I yearned through six-stanza lines I learned from you.

You spent January of your last winter
up on that mountain.

I love a boy who died and a girl who left.
I love a brother who is a grown woman.
I love your eight books. I hate the ending.
I never knew you.

You knew a lot about airports and rivers
and a girl who went away in October.
Fathers, brothers and sisters die of cancer:
still, we are strangers.

You are the lonely gathering of rivers
below the plane that left you in Ohio;
you are the fog of language on Manhattan
where it's descending.

Marilyn Hacker

Donald Hall (b. 1928)

Names of Curtains*

after Donald Hall

All day by sheer fullness you strained
against the light, crossing and ruffle
spinning casement onto ledge.
In April you framed the dandelions'
organdy heads and cheered
the violet rain. All summer
you curved while the lawn mower's
back and forth paths dried and faded.
Sundays you lightly waited
while we read the heavy Times
smoothing the shard-filled glass.
When you were limp and gray one late October
the woman who washed and ironed you,
fussed a little with you every morning;
took you down, shook out your dust
and the last of your warm cotton smell.
That night through the hedges with sticky
ghosts and silly brides you fled.

O festoon, jabot, swag, puff, tieback, crescent, Priscilla.

Nola Garrett

*See Hall's "Names of Horses."

Ted Hughes (b. 1930)

A Policeman's Lot*

> The progress of any writer is marked by those moments when he
> manages to outwit his own inner police system. —Ted Hughes

Oh, once I was a policeman young and merry (young and merry),
Controlling crowds and fighting petty crime (petty crime),
But now I work on matters literary (litererry)
And I am growing old before my time ('fore my time).
No, the imagination of a writer (of a writer)
Is not the sort of beat a chap would choose (chap would choose)
And they've assigned me a prolific blighter ('lific blighter)—
I'm patrolling the unconscious of Ted Hughes.

It's not the sort of beat a chap would choose (chap would choose)—
Patrolling the unconscious of Ted Hughes.

All our leave was cancelled in the lambing season (lambing season),
When bitter winter froze the drinking trough (drinking trough),
For our commander stated, with good reason (with good reason),
That that's the kind of thing that starts him off (starts him off).
But anything with four legs causes trouble (causes trouble)—
It's worse than organizing several zoos (several zoos),
Not to mention mythic creatures in the rubble (in the rubble),
Patrolling the unconscious of Ted Hughes.

It's worse than organizing several zoos (several zoos)—
Patrolling the unconscious of Ted Hughes.

Although it's disagreeable and stressful (bull and stressful)
Attempting to avert poetic thought ('etic thought),
I could boast of times when I have been successful (been successful)
And conspiring compound epithets were caught ('thets were caught).

But the poetry statistics in this sector (in this sector)
Are enough to make a copper turn to booze (turn to booze)
And I do not think I'll make it to inspector (to inspector)
Patrolling the unconscious of Ted Hughes.

It's enough to make a copper turn to booze (turn to booze)—
Patrolling the unconscious of Ted Hughes.

after W.S. Gilbert
Wendy Cope

*The poem follows the form of "A Policeman's Lot Is Not a Happy One" from Gilbert and
Sullivan's *The Pirates of Penzance*.

Yevgeny Yevtushenko (b. 1933)

To Yevtushenko

My dove-gray brother,
behaving as poets are supposed to behave,
as Russians are supposed to,
enunciating your language in your whole body
and all over the stage,
hand to heart,
I am entranced.
Is it all so simple?

My brother from the City of Yes,
why would you be a woman only once, for a moment?
Is it so narrow for women in Russia?
Your voice rolls out
like thunder from the Grand Canyon,
deep as water cuts cliffs.
I haven't such powers,
my virtues more like tears.

Dear dwarf birch tree,
if the climate has oppressed you,
you have also toughened,
bent to the very edge
and sprung back,
a resilience almost feminine.

Judith Bishop

But You Were Not at Babii Yar, Mr. Yevtushenko*

You are very aware.
You cry for all the victims.
You imagine yourself
Anne Frank, but she wasn't there,
and you are not a woman.

For all your anguish
you could only empathize.
You never felt the
insult of a bullet,
never fell into that ravine,
never felt the snow
in your mouth mix with blood,
never saw the light go
permanently dark.

Nor did you lose a family member
or a friend into that
yawn of time.
You were always safe, always fed.

For me the ghosts are real,
and when, at last, I stood in the snow,
above that ordinary split of earth,
I heard them hiss their final breath.

You wrote of national death.
I mourn the loss of Anna, Mary,
Harry, Sammy, David, Rachel, Saul,
Joseph: my family. Nothing political—
simply a very complicated, irremeable loss.

Barbara Brent Brower

*See Yevtushenko's "Babii Yar."

Mark Strand (b. 1934)

Mark Strand

the first time
it is safer

to read
his poetry

the second time
i am split

holding the book
hearing myself

read to me
the third time

i fear
i am

on the train
engineered

by him
running himself

over
the rails.

Naomi Rachel

Joseph Brodsky (1940-1996)

Brodsky

First the words in English,
ragged. I listen,
as though through a hotel wall,
hawks climb to the ionosphere
where he dissolves into snow.
Then the Russian.
We're off,
orbs of sounds flying
from your hooves like packed snow,
voice chanting higher and higher.
I don't know what it's about
but the excitement
stops suddenly, brakes,
and you turn back to your chair.

Judith Bishop

Tom Disch (b. 1940)

*Riposte**

<pre>
                    (I never could
        Figure out how anyone can justify poetry
        As a full-time job. How do they get through
        The day at MacDowell—filling out
        Applications for the next free lunch?)
                    —Tom Disch: "Working on a Tan"
</pre>

Dear Tom,
         When my next volume (granted: slender)
is granted an advance of more than two
thou, perhaps I'll scorn all grants and spend a
couple of them on summer rent, like you,

in the right Hampton with the novelists
who swap Hollywood options with bravado.
Their *au pairs* hoard handwritten shopping-lists;
their word-processors go with them to Yaddo

where novelists are still *persona grata,*
nor do their royalties or last advance
cause the *per diem* charge to rise *pro rata.*
I'd ever so much rather be in France

and not have to eat dinner at six-thirty
with frozen carrots and Kraft's French (*sic*) Dressing.
But potshotting "free-lunch" is playing dirty;
successful applicants should count their blessings.

I wouldn't want the kitchen staff to brand me
an ingrate who will bite the hand that feeds me
if I am going to eat the food they hand me
—and they're in the minority that reads me.

Is poetry a full-time occupation?
Practitioners have spliced it with exciting
alternative careers in transportation
—drive cabs, that is—or teach Creative Writing

or First-Year French or Freshman Composition,
translate, wait tables, sell insurance, edit.
If "poet" 's written where it says: PROFESSION:
American Express extends no credit.

And you see no excuse for poets' lives
because we're paid so mingily; that's it?
I think of "unemployed" mothers, housewives
whose work was judged equivalent to shit-

shoveling on Frank Perdue's chicken farm
by gents who calibrate Job Equity.
All that they are today they owe to Mom!
Do novelists owe shit to poetry?

SF writer snipes poets on the pages
of *Poetry:* that's also aiming low,
though nowhere near as low as poets' wages.
At fifty cents a line, where would *you* go?

And fifty cents a line's exemplary!
Measure it to your last *Playboy* short-short
and you might find an artist's colony
a perfectly respectable resort.

Marilyn Hacker

*Disch's poem first appeared in *Poetry* and is collected in his *Yes, Let's: New and Selected Poems.*

Michael Ryan (b. 1946)

I Ask Myself if This Is the Start of a Prose Poem

I ask myself if I will write a letter to Michael Ryan
who just won the Yale and is nominated for the National
Book Award. It would be a sensuous letter because I cried
when I read some of his poetry and because I felt despair
when I didn't and because I wonder if mine is as good.
Then I consider that it may be an egocentric business letter
because he is sure to be a major poet and wouldn't it be good
for him to know my name. After all, I know his. And then the picture
on the jacket is appealing in an American way. But then I have to
ask myself what the hell could I say to him after all if I don't even
know if this is a prose poem.

Naomi Rachel

Anonymous (Contemporary)

Winning the Prize

There he is one morning when I open my door
after all these years, after twelve years,
spread flat across the brown carpet
of my hall with all the other newspapers,
staring from the cover of the *New York Times*
with the same overgrown moustache and droopy eyes
that he had when I took his class,
when I was so young I didn't have a voice,
when I wasn't able to ask a bus driver for a transfer
or a woman in a shop with clinking jewelry for change,
when I never got over my shock from the man who fell
to my feet in the subway and said *"I want to be your love slave,"*
or the man on Eighth Street who asked for my last five dollars
and it seemed like a fair deal when he sang an aria,
when I thought everyone in the street was shouting
"I know who you are, you don't belong here,"
when I didn't have much but I spent what I had
on tuition and books, and I didn't always have food,
and I sat in the poetry class of this man
who now soaks up ink from the *Times,*
who just won the Pulitzer Prize,
who would stand in front of the class
during dark November afternoons
with his leg up on a chair,
who would saunter through the room
like a man who never lost his way in the world,
his red cowboy boots hitting the linoleum floor
as I held my breath too terrified to speak,
when he would rest his hand on my shoulder,
when he once whispered with a sea-washed voice
so softly that I could barely hear the words:

"What would it be like if we made love?"
and I would look up into his eyes, stuff my voice
down my throat, swallow saliva, and say nothing,
and I never answered the question, never considered the question,
but I thought what I could do,
what I could say to the chairman of the department
whose glasses pinched his nose, who always spoke in quotes,
who might lean back in his chair with his legs up on his desk
and shrug his shoulders and say nothing,
and I knew even then
that this is the way things are:
men win the big prizes
and what women get
is an arm around the waist from a passing stranger,
a hand resting on the top of the head,
a soft voice in the ear asking what it would be like.

Penny Cagan

The Perfect Poet

He says he is a perfect poet.
He lives alone, with his perfect mate.
& sometimes they don't even speak,
So perfectly do they "communicate."

He lives alone, his greatest pleasures are
His pipes, his books, his wife's behind—
Which he will often pinch to hear her laugh;
He's got a perfect love for womankind.

He seldom writes, distrusting language as
A clumsy tool, unequal to his thoughts:
He uses it as rarely as he can
(No doubt to punish it for all its faults).

But when he writes, he keeps the upper hand
(On principle, since words are enemies).
He melts them down, then counterfeits his own—
A kind of literary alchemy.

He's fortunate to have a perfect muse.
A live-in muse, who cooks inspiringly;
And sometimes after an ambrosial meal,
He'll grab his pen, composing feverishly

A perfect poem, describing in detail
The salad, wine, the roast in buttery baste.
And reading it, his musing wife agrees
That every lines smacks of his perfect taste.

Erica Jong

Going Down on America: The Regional Poet

Turned on to the transcendent, he holds her
in his arms, strokes her sunny hair.
Such sweet skin is coming into view
as the clothes of Straight are shed
over New Jersey & kicked aside
into the wide Missouri River—

He pledges allegiance to lightfilled breasts,
to the drops of shine spilled
on Shenandoah's applerich harvest.

In this union of smoke & suck he enters a state just west
of grace where Wyoming is what cowboys do
on Saturday night when the boss has paid them up
& the wind smells of Montana carried downstream,
clean but unmistakable.

O Mount Rushmore,
move him to your eyes of stone!

In wheat fields he may dream
of stalks of sun,

discover blue shadows
in the shingles of the fallen pinecone!

The seventh day dawns somewhere above the fabulous Sierras
& in a whirlwind of contradiction funnels itself south
into the dusk of his throat,
enlightens his heart,
& sets the flesh to dancing upon bare bones
across known borders
into a land lost
to reality.

Kelly Cherry

Erato Erratum

You say I am your prism and your muse:
My eyes inspire you to work and live;
You filter ideas through me, and my views
Refine yours, as if I were a sieve.
And what of me? Who models for my art?
Who bandages my heart when it is sore?
A pussycat mews—is that to be my part?
And what if I refuse, a muse no more?
The graces are always women, never men,
So on my pedestal I stand, with itching toes
Posing as Mother Mary or as Magdalen,
And wondering how you look without your clothes.
By candlelight, my dear, I pick your brains;
When I'm alone, I put you in quatrains.

Verna Safran

What It Must Be Like for Certain Wives to Read Their Well-Known Husbands' Poetry

A man lusts after his wife's young cousin,
having come upon her changing
from her bathing suit in the master bedroom.
He describes her tanned body, marvels
at the strips the sun has missed. Worse,
he thinks he deserves this girl's
sixteen-year-old flesh. He combs his hair
over a balding spot in his author's photo
on the back of his book. (How could any reader resist
a mid-poem look?) The poet stares back, his thick
coke-bottle glasses magnifying his earnestness.
He concludes his narrative with a whine,
his aging body misrepresenting his drive.
Perhaps he swears to his wife, "You don't understand!
I create art. Your cousin? I never thought
about her twice." Maybe the wife's hurt is so deep
that she hasn't the strength
to use the arsenic she buys to kill him
and places it, instead, on a shelf for herself.
Another poet drools over his freshman students
who he's convinced are torturing him
with their cashmere sweaters. He dismisses
their complaints of harassment, concocting
a penile metaphor, comparing his sex
to a harmless link of breakfast food.
The tone, if forced, is omelette-fluffy.
His wincing wife, not wanting to be accused
of being a poor sport, decides never
to bring up the subject of the poem. Another woman
fears it isn't she in her husband's sonnet.
She doesn't have the kind of inverted nipples he praises.
The perfume, the hotel are all wrong.
Rather than hear again that he is more
than a confessional poet, she takes

a lover of her own, then paints
his eyes on the world's largest canvas.
A different wife must face the explanation
of the affair. Her husband's poor typeset excuse:
his dying mother and career stress, the childhood flashback—
his absentee father, a cold snowflake.
This wife meets our first wife at a conference,
or possibly the supermarket. They exchange stories,
their husbands' lousy teaching jobs, the tedious readings
they've had to sit through. They're sick
of the weakness of the male spirit. Why must they endure
public humiliation without at least fur coats or tropical vacations?
The two women start the beginnings of a good plot.
Our first wife decides to flush the arsenic
and live. Her husband doesn't deserve
any raw material that good.

Yvette Carbeaux

Tumps

Don't ask him the time of day. He won't know it,
For he's the abstracted sort.
In fact, he's a typically useless male poet.
We'll call him a tump for short.

A tump isn't punctual or smart or efficient,
He probably can't drive a car
Or follow a map, though he's very proficient
At finding his way to the bar.

He may have great talent, and not just for writing—
For drawing, or playing the drums.
But don't let him loose on accounts—that's inviting
Disaster. A tump can't do sums.

He cannot get organized. Just watch him try it
And you'll see a frustrated man.
But some tumps (and these are the worst ones) deny it
And angrily tell you they can.

I used to be close to a tump who would bellow
"You think I can't add two and two!"
And get even crosser when, smiling and mellow,
I answered, "You're quite right. I do."

Women poets are businesslike, able,
Good drivers, and right on the ball,
And some of us still know our seven times table.
We're not like the tumps. Not at all.

Wendy Cope

and VICE VERSA

Dialectic

Impotent

His malady at root was sexual,
His explanation intellectual

                      Perhaps, my dear, the fault was dual.
                      But to say any more were cruel.

Riposte

The fault was dual?
Certainly not.
It's as simple as plumbing—
The cold can't run hot.

                      As simple as plumbing?
                      A man has his pride.
                      A faucet can't work
                      When there's nothing inside.

Nancy Winters   *Bruce Bennett*

Contributors' Notes

B.B. ADAMS
has published two books of poems, *Hapax Legomena* (Edwin Mellen Press) and *Double Solitaire* (Geryon Press) and a book of literary criticism, *The Enemy Self: Poetry and Criticism of Laura Riding* (UMI/University of Rochester Presses). Her poems, stories, and critical essays have appeared in a wide variety of publications, and she gives many readings for colleges and arts councils. She is a Professor of English at Pace University in New York City.

ANNA AKHMATOVA (1889–1966)
was born in Odessa, Russia, and lived most of her life in Leningrad. Her first two poetry books, *Vecher* ("Evening," 1912) and *Chyotki* ("Rosary," 1914) brought her fame, and she was associated with the Akmeists, who eschewed Symbolist vagueness in favor of clarity, simplicity, and formal skill. From 1922–1940, and again from 1946–1959, she was silenced as a poet by the Soviet regime. In 1921 her former husband, poet Nikolay Gumilyov, was executed; in 1934 her second husband, Osip Mandelstamm, died in (or en route to) a labor camp; in 1946 her son was imprisoned, to be released only after Stalin's death. In the last years of her life, Akhmatova's work was again permitted to appear in Soviet periodicals. Her collected poems were published in 1965, the same year in which she received an honory degree from Oxford University.

RONNIE APTER
is Associate Professor of English at Central Michigan University and author of *Digging for Treasure: Translation After Pound*. She is translating the lyrics of the troubadour Bernart de Vantadorn and, in collaboration with Mark Herman, has translated fifteen operas performed in the United States, Canada, and England.

MARGARET ATWOOD
is the author of more than twenty books, including poetry, novels, short story collections, and literary criticism. Among her collections of poetry are *Selected Poems* (Simon & Schuster), *Two-Headed Poems* (Oxford University Press), and *True Stories* (Jonathan Cape). The recipient of many awards for her writing, Atwood lives in Toronto with the novelist Graeme Gibson and their daughter, Jess.

GRACE BAUER
has published two chapbooks of poems: *Where You've Seen Her* (Pennywhistle Press)

and *The House Where I've Never Lived* (Anabiosis Press). Her work has also appeared in a variety of journals, including *Poetry, New Orleans Review,* and *Southern Poetry Review.* She teaches Creative Writing at the University of Nebraska.

BRUCE BENNETT

has the distinction of being the sole male contributor to this volume (in dialogue with Nancy Winters). His poetry appears widely in periodicals and anthologies; in addition to several chapbooks, he has published two full-length poetry collections: *Straw into Gold* (Cleveland State, 1984) and *Taking Off* (Orchises, 1992). He is Professor of English and director of the creative writing program at Wells, a women's college in Aurora, New York.

TONI LA REE BENNETT

has been writing since 1975 while raising twin sons and working. Returning to college in 1984, she received her B.A., M.A., and Ph.D. from the University of Washington-Seattle, where she taught English part-time for five years. She has written magazine articles, a Western novel, and short stories, edited a literary magazine, assisted in preparing a Medieval drama anthology, and worked as a news correspondent. She has recently completed a chapbook of poems based on New Zealand. Future plans include spending more time in Italy and translating the work of contemporary Italian poets.

MAXIANNE BERGER,

an audiologist, lives in Montréal, Québec. Her poetry has appeared in Canadian literary magazines and anthologies, including *Bywords, Zymergy,* and the League of Canadian Poets' *Vintage 94.* Her American credits include a short short story in *Homage to a RedWheelbarrow,* and poems in *Grasslands Review* and online in *DeepBreath.* She has recently completed an M.A. in English Literature at Concordia University.

JUDITH BISHOP

is from New England and New York City but has lived in California for the past eighteen years. She received her writing degree from Columbia, winning the Academy of American Poets University Prize upon graduation. She started her own press in New York City, taught writing and literature in New Hampshire, and worked as a symphonic violinist in Maine. In California she has been an editor for *Coastlight,* a poetry anthology, and for WPA, a local press. Her poetry has appeared in various magazines and anthologies and has won many awards. In 1994 her first full book, *The Burning Place* (Fithian Press) and a small book of meditations, *Wheel of Breath,* were published. She has recently completed *Snow Mountain,* poems from 1991-95, and is compiling another collection, *Walking Into Each Other.*

KATHLEEN BOGAN

is a cousin of Louise Bogan and studied with Donald Justice. Her work appears in *Seattle Review, Alaska Quarterly Review, Writers' Forum, Confrontation,* and other journals. An exhibiting artist and lawyer as well as an award-winning poet, she makes her home in Portland, Oregon.

LOUISE BOGAN (1897–1970)

published four books of poetry and is equally acclaimed for her acute literary criticism, most notably in *Achievement in American Poetry,* a survey of U.S. poetry in the first half of the twentieth century. She served for many years as poetry editor for *The New Yorker,* taught at several universities, and held the chair of poetry at the Library of Congress. Bogan was the recipient of the Bollingen Prize in Poetry and an award from the Academy of American Poets; in 1968 she was elected a member of the American Academy of Arts and Letters. *What the Woman Knew,* published in 1974, is a collection of her letters.

ANNE BRADSTREET (c. 1612–1672)

belonged to one of the founding families of the Massachusetts Bay Colony. Her poetry was composed amid the hardships of early Colonial life, the responsibilities of raising eight children, many physical illnesses, and serving as hostess for her husband and father, both high government officials in the colony. Bradstreet's book of poems was first published in England as *The Tenth Muse Lately Sprung Up in America* (1650); the American edition, published posthumously in 1678, was titled *Several Poems Compiled with Great Variety of Wit and Learning.* In her more personal poems, she wrote movingly of awaiting childbirth, her relationship with her husband, and the destruction of her house by fire. Other work explores her spiritual growth as she struggled with the Puritan creed. Her metaphysical poems have been compared to those of Donne.

BARBARA BRENT BROWER

was born in Chicago and educated at The Art Institute of Chicago, Corcoran School of Art, and George Washington University. She lived in Washington, DC, for twenty years, where she raised her three children, and now resides in Okemos, Michigan. More than two hundred of her poems have been published in magazines and literary journals, and she has won several awards, most recently from the Poetry Society of Georgia/Coca-Cola Company/Olympics. She has served as president of the Lansing Poetry Club and the Poetry Society of Michigan.

LINDA CARTER BROWN

was born in South Carolina and moved to Miami, Florida, at the age of eight. She lived in New York City for twenty-seven years, where she attended NYU and the

City University of the City of New York. She began writing poetry at the age of forty.

PENNY CAGAN

was born in Trenton, New Jersey. She earned a Master of Arts degree in Creative Writing from NYU and a Master of Library Science degree from Rutger's University. Her undergraduate education was completed at the University of Rochester, and she spent her junior year abroad at the University of Edinburgh. Her work has appeared in many journals and anthologies, including *What's Become of Eden: Poems of the Family* (Slapering Hol Press), *The New York Quarterly, Calyx, Earth's Daughters, The California State Poetry Quarterly, The Jewish Spectator,* and *The Lancashire Poetry Review.* She works as a reference librarian in New York City.

YVETTE CARBEAUX

has published fiction in such magazines as *Mangrove.* This book marks her debut as a published poet.

PHOEBE CARY (1824–1871)

is most remembered for her parodies and other humorous poems, which are still often found in anthologies of light verse. She published several poetry collections of her own and several others in collaboration with her sister, Alice Cary; all are long out of print.

KELLY CHERRY's

books include the poetry collections *God's Loud Hand, Natural Theology, Relativity: A Point of View,* and *Lovers and Agnostics,* and the poetry chapbooks *Songs for a Soviet Composer, Benjamin John,* and *Time Out of Mind.* She has also published five novels and the autobiographical narrative *The Exiled Heart.* A new book of poetry, *Death and Transfiguration,* is forthcoming in 1997.

KATHARINE COLES

has published two collections of poetry, *The One Right Touch* (Ahsahta Press, 1992) and *A History of the Garden* (University of Nevada, 1997). She is also the author of a novel, *The Measurable World* (University of Nevada, 1995). She lives in Salt Lake City, Utah.

JANE COOPER

grew up in Jacksonville, Florida, and Princeton, New Jersey. Her first book of poems, *The Weather of Six Mornings,* received the Lamont Award in 1968. *Maps and Windows* appeared in 1978 and *Scaffolding: New and Selected Poems* in 1984. In 1978 she was co-recipient of the Shelley Award from the Poetry Society of America. She lives in New York City.

WENDY COPE

was born in Erinth, Kent and educated at St. Hilda's College, Oxford. After university she worked for fifteen years as a primary school teacher in London. Her collections of poetry include *Making Cocoa for Kingsley Amis* (1986) and *Serious Concerns* (1992), both published by Faber and Faber. She now lives in Hampshire, where she works as a freelance writer and editor.

ENID DAME

is a poet, writer, and teacher whose work has appeared in many publications, including *New York Quarterly, Negative Capability, Tikkun,* and *Fiction.* Her latest book of poems is *Anything You Don't See* (Albuquerque, NM: West End Press, 1992). She teaches creative writing at Rutgers University and was a finalist in the recent search for Poet Laureate of Brooklyn, where she lives much of the time.

GRAY DAVIS

has published poems in recent issues of *Calyx* and *Exquisite Corpse.* She lives in the Sangre de Cristo mountains outside Glorieta, New Mexico.

KAREN DONNELLY

is co-editor, with J.B. Bernstein, of *Our Mothers Our Selves: Writers and Poets Celebrating Motherhood.* Her poems have been published in *Earth's Daughters, Hawaii Review,* and elsewhere. She shares her Bethany, Connecticut, home with her husband, David, and her daughters Cathy and Colleen, who like to see their names in print.

DIANE ENGLE

is an attorney by education and a musician (organ and piano) and writer by profession. She has published poetry in numerous journals in the United States, Canada, and the U.K., including *The Formalist, Sparrow, Pearl,* and *Queen's Quarterly.* Her prose work, dealing with the subjects of adoption and education, has appeared in magazines, newspapers, and anthologies.

RHINA P. ESPAILLAT

was born in the Dominican Republic in 1932 and has lived in the U.S. since 1939. She writes chiefly in English but occasionally in her native Spanish. Her work has been included in numerous anthologies and appears regularly in poetry magazines, most recently *Poetry, Hellas, Tennessee Quarterly, Pivot,* and *Poetry Digest.* A collection of her poems, *Lapsing to Grace,* was published by Bennett & Kitchell.

PAT FALK

teaches English at Nassau Community College in New York. Her writing has appeared in several poetry, literary, and feminist journals, and a volume of her poems,

In the Shape of a Woman, was recently published by Canio's Editions, Sag Harbor, New York. She is currently working on a book of feminist poetics, titled *The Feminization of Form.*

BETH FEIN
has published poetry in *The Long Island Quarterly, Bay Windows, Poetpourri,* and *5x7.* She is currently at work on a manuscript entitled *Only One Name for Red.* She is employed as a graphic designer in New York City.

ANNIE FINCH's
poems have appeared in many journals, including *The Kenyon Review, Southwest Review, Paris Review,* and elsewhere, and her forthcoming book of poems, *Changing-Woman,* was a finalist in the National Poetry Series and the Yale Series of Younger Poets. She has written a book of literary theory, *The Ghost of Meter: Culture and Prosody in American Free Verse* (University of Michigan Press), and edited two anthologies, *A Formal Feeling Comes: Poems in Form by Contemporary Women* (Story Line Press) and *Beyond New Formalism: New Essays on Poetic Form and Narrative* (Story Line, forthcoming). Currently on the creative writing faculty at Miami University in Ohio, she earned her B.A. at Yale and her Doctorate at Stanford University.

ERICA-LYNN GAMBINO
is a painter and writer, born in New York in 1969. She received her B.A. from NYU and her M.A. from Bennington College. Her poems and stories have been published in *Minetta Review, SILO,* and *QUIX Art Quarterly.* She currently lives on Long Island, where she works as a columnist for the *Southampton Press,* continues to paint, and works on her second novel, various articles and essays, and a book of short stories. She dedicates her poem in this anthology to Lorie Hartman.

NOLA GARRETT
lives in Spring Hill, Florida, and directs a creative writing workshop for the Hernando County Library. Her poems have appeared in *Poet Lore, Flyaway, Christian Century, Yellow Silk, The Formalist, The Georgia Review,* and *Odd Angles of Heaven,* edited by David Craig and Janet McCann. She has been awarded a scholarship to the White River Writers' Workshop and a fellowship to Yaddo.

CHANDA J. GLASS
received her Master's Degree in English from New Mexico State University. Fascinated by Greek mythology since third grade, she was piqued that the stories of its women were either told by men or ignored completely. Her first book of poetry, *Alecto's Sisters,* attempts a remedy.

JULIA GOLDBERG

makes her living as a freelance journalist in Santa Fe, New Mexico. She holds a Master's Degree in Creative Writing from the University of New Mexico and is currently at work on a novel.

MARILYN HACKER

has won the National Book Award, fellowships from the Guggenheim and Ingram Merrill Foundations, and the Lamont Poetry Award. She is the author of *Presentation Piece; Separations; Love, Death and the Changing of the Seasons; Going Back to the River;* and *Winter Numbers.* Her *Selected Poems: 1965-1990* won the Poet's Prize. A former editor of *13th Moon* and *The Kenyon Review,* she lives in New York and Paris.

BARBARA HARR (1937–1995)

was born in Nigeria to American missionary parents. She was educated at the University of Chicago and taught English at Loyola University and Upsala College. In addition to a volume of poetry, *The Mortgaged Wife,* she wrote lyrics for contemporary hymns and was one of the leading American breeders of Javanese cats. At the time of her death she was completing a Ph.D. at Garrett-Evangelical Theological Seminary in Evanston, Illinois.

ANN HAYES

has been writing and publishing poetry since 1942. Her *Letters at Christmas and Other Poems* (Badger Press, Pittsburgh, PA, 1995) is a collection of fifty years' work, most of it published earlier in serial form and in other books. She is a professor of English at Carnegie Mellon University in Pittsburgh, where she has taught for many years. She has also taught at Stanford University, Indiana University, and Coe College.

H.D. (1886–1961)

was born Hilda Doolittle in Pennsylvania but lived in Europe from 1911 until her death, and from the time of her first published work was known as H.D. to both readers and acquaintances. She was an early member of the Imagist movement and an admirer of Sappho; though she later disassociated herself from the Imagists, her poetry continued to exhibit the clarity, directness, and precision that were Imagist principles and is also characteristic of Sappho's work. H.D. wrote numerous volumes of poetry, essays, novels, a play, translations of Greek drama, and two memoirs: one about her early relationship with Pound, the other about her psychoanalysis with Freud.

DOROTHY HICKSON

is a recovering English major (Wellesley, 1990) who now lives in the Adams-Morgan neighborhood of Washington, D.C. She is currently working on her first novel.

MARY HOLTBY

was born in Oxford, England, and attended that university. She taught English, Latin, and Classical Studies in various schools and worked as Research Assistant on the University of California's edition of Donne's sermons. She has contributed comic verse to several anthologies and written libretti for two children's operas. Her children's opera *Caedmon,* with music by Richard Shephard, premiered in July 1996 at the York Early Music Festival. She and her husband live in Yorkshire.

KATHLEEN IDDINGS

resides in La Jolla, California. West Anglia published her fourth book, *Selected and New Poems, 1980-1990,* and she has been the recipient of an NEA/COMBO Fellowship, Djerassi Artists' Colony Residency, and PEN and Carnegie Writers' Grants. More than three hundred and fifty of her poems have appeared in such places as McGraw Hill's college textbook *Literature,* Fields's *A New Geography of Poets,* Pater's *Yearbook of American Poetry,* and numerous journals. She is editor and publisher of San Diego Poet's Press and La Jolla Press, which have published five anthologies and thirty books by individual poets. The presses also sponsor national book contests: the American Book Series and National Poetry Series.

ESTHER JOHNSON (1681–1728)

met Jonathan Swift in 1689, when he went to live in the Moor Park home of Sir William Temple, where her mother was housekeeper. In 1701 she moved to Dublin with her companion, Rebecca Dingley, and lived there the rest of her life. Her death, after many years of painful illness, so devastated Swift that he was unable to attend her funeral, but he later wrote a memoir in her praise. His poems to "Stella," as he called her, are among the most charming love poems ever written. Despite some speculation that the two were secretly married, there is no conclusive evidence that their relationship was other than platonic.

ERICA JONG

has published more than a dozen books, including poetry, fiction, and non-fiction. Her most recently published poetry collection, *Becoming Light: New and Selected Poems* (HarperCollins, 1991), contains work from seven previous books, in addition to many early and recent poems. Jong lives in Connecticut, New York, and Vermont with her husband and daughter.

MARGARET KAY

received a degree (summa cum laude) from the University of Massachusetts at Boston at the age of 71. She was the first recipient of a Ragdale Fellowship for Older Women. Her poetry has appeared in *The American Scholar, Boston Phoenix, Negative Capability, Visions International,* and *Worcester Review.* Her book of poems, based on the letters and journals of Cornelia Dixon, a woman living on Indian Island in the mid-1800s, is currently seeking a publisher.

ALINE KILMER (1888–1941)

was the wife of Joyce Kilmer, author of "Trees." Her own poetry, at its best, is reminiscent of Elinor Wylie's in its technical skill, directness, depth of feeling, and absence of sentimentality. Kilmer's poetry collections included *Candles that Burn* (1919), *The Poor King's Daughter, and Other Poems* (1925), and *Selected Poems* (1929).

CAROLYN KIZER

is the author of eight books of poems (including a book of translations), the most recent being *Harping On: Poems 1985-1995* (Copper Canyon, 1996). She has published two books of essays on poetry and prose, and has edited *The Essential John Clare* and *100 Great Poems by Women* (both Ecco Press). Her poetry collection *Yin* (BOA Editions, 1984) was awarded the Pulitzer Prize.

YALA KORWIN,

a former Art Librarian, is the author of *To Tell the Story—Poems of the Holocaust* (U.S. Holocaust Memorial Museum, Washington, DC). Several of her poems are anthologized in *Blood to Remember* (Ch. Fishman, ed.), *Sarah's Daughters Sing* (H. Wenkart, ed.), *Anthology of Magazine Verse 1986-88* (A.F. Pater, ed.), and in the forthcoming *Patchwork of Dreams* (M. Sklar, ed.). She is also a visual, exhibiting artist.

JOYCE LA MERS,

a Montana native, lives in Oxnard, California, where she and her husband run a small manufacturing business. Her poetry, much of it light verse, has appeared in national publications including *Light, Saturday Evening Post, REAL, Poets On, Amelia, Piedmont Literary Review,* and in several anthologies. Her collection of poems, *Grandma Rationalizes an Enthusiasm for Skydiving,* is a 1996 publication from Mille Grazie Press.

PEGGY LANDSMAN

lives in Albany, California. Her poems have appeared in several literary magazines, including *The Tomcat, The Liberty Hill Poetry Review,* and *Calyx.* She is indebted to many Muses but lusts after one in particular, whose name is Richard.

EMILIA (BASSANO) LANIER (1569–1645)

was a highly skilled poet and independent thinker whose long work, *Salve Deus Rex Judaeorum* (1611) offers sympathetic, revisionist portraits of biblical women and of Cleopatra. Some scholars believe that she was the Dark Lady of Shakespeare's Sonnets 127–152. Lanier, who was married to a court musician at the time those poems were written, is said to have been insulted by Shakespeare's portrayal of her.

JEAN LEBLANC

lives in rural New Jersey, where she writes poetry, fiction, reviews, and creative non-fiction. Reading, bird watching, and walking in the woods are a few of her sources of inspiration. Her work has appeared in *Earth's Daughters, The Lullwater Review,* and *Classical Digest.*

RACHEL LODEN's
poem "My Night with Philip Larkin" also appeared in *The Best American Poetry 1995* (Simon & Schuster). Her poetry has been published in *Antioch Review, Boulevard, New American Writing,* and many other magazines, as well as the anthology *American Poets Say Goodbye to the 20th Century.* She writes and teaches in Palo Alto, California.

BARBARA LOOTS
earns her keep as a writer for Hallmark Cards. On the side, she writes poems which have appeared in numerous literary and general magazines, including *The Lyric, Helicon Nine, New Letters, The Formalist, Blue Unicorn,* and *The Christian Century.* Recent anthologies include *The Random House Treasury of Light Verse* and *Holy Humor.* Her chapbooks are *The Bride's Mirror Speaks* and, with Gail White, *Sibyl & Sphinx.* She is a member of the adjunct faculty of Baker University.

AMY LOWELL (1874–1925)
was a member of the distinguished Lowell family of Boston. She began devoting herself to poetry at age twenty-eight and published her first book in 1914. Her second volume, *Sword Blades and Poppy Seed,* included the first poems in English to combine free and formal verse, which she termed "polyphonic prose." Lowell was known for her powerful personality, independence, and disdain for social conventions. When she displaced Ezra Pound as leader of the Imagist movement, he began referring to those poets as "Amygists." Lowell published eight volumes of poetry, translations of Chinese and Japanese poetry, critical studies, and a two-volume biography of Keats; she was also a popular lecturer. A posthumous book of poems, *What's O'Clock,* was awarded the Pulitzer Prize.

CATHERINE MARTIN
has published poems in *5x7* and *The Salmon* (Galway, Ireland). Currently she is on leave from the MFA Writing Program at Vermont College to work on her manuscript, "Bellydancing in the Stacks," and to explore the Northwest. She recently moved to Seattle from New York City.

KATHERINE MCALPINE
lives in the island village of Eastport, Maine. Her poetry has appeared in many periodicals, including *The Nation, The Formalist, Sparrow, Hellas, The Dark Horse,* and *Cumberland Poetry Review,* and in several textbooks and anthologies, most recently *Literature: The Human Experience* (St. Martin's, 1997). She has been the Featured Poet in *Light* and *The Epigrammatist;* her awards for poetry include the "Discovery"/*The Nation* Award and the Judith's Room Award for emerging women poets.

PHYLLIS MCGINLEY (1905–1978)

was one of the 20th century's most skilled and prolific writers of light verse, which frequently cast a satiric eye on American suburban life. She credited Katharine S. White of *The New Yorker* with encouraging and supporting her early career, and her poetry appeared frequently in that magazine for many years. McGinley also published serious poetry and numerous children's books. Her collection *Times Three: Selected Verse from Three Decades* won the Pulitzer Prize in 1961.

CAROL E. MILLER

received her Ph.D. in English, with a creative writing concentration, from the University of Wisconsin-Milwaukee. She is the recipient of the 1995 Hart Crane Award for poetry, a 1996 Robert Penn Warren Poetry Prize, and has published poems in numerous journals. Her essay "Toward an Alternative Formalist Tradition" is forthcoming in *Beyond New Formalism* (Story Line Press), edited by Annie Finch. She teaches in the Liberal Arts Department of the School of the Art Institute of Chicago.

LADY MARY WORTLEY MONTAGU (1689–1762)

was celebrated during her lifetime as a poet, essayist, and a prolific writer of witty, eloquent letters. An early, outspoken feminist, she eloped with Edward Wortley Montagu, a member of Parliament, rather than agree to a marriage arranged by her father. She was a friend of such literary figures as Addison, Steele, Voltaire, Fielding (a second cousin), Gay, and Pope, though Pope later turned against her. (For an account of their quarrel, see the note to her poem "Verses Address'd to the Imitator of the First Satire of the Second Book of Horace.") In addition to her literary achievements, she introduced the practice of smallpox inoculation into England after having observed the process in Turkey.

KEL MUNGER

lives and works in Ames, Iowa. She spent eight years as a 911-Dispatcher/Jailor with the Ames Police Department, recently leaving the position to accept the Pearl Hogrefe Fellowship in Creative Writing at Iowa State University. She is currently working on an M.A. in literature. Her poems have appeared in *Sinister Wisdom, Lynx Eye,* and *Iowa Woman.*

SHARON OLDS

was born in San Francisco and educated at Stanford University and Columbia University. Her books of poetry include *Satan Says, The Dead and the Living* (a Lamont Poetry Selection and winner of the National Book Critics Circle Award), *The Gold Cell,* and *The Father.* She teaches poetry workshops in the Graduate Creative Writing Program at NYU and at Goldwater Hospital on Roosevelt Island in New York.

JUNE OWENS

reviews books for *Amelia, The Blue Penny Quarterly, The Chattahoochee Review,* and *The Unforgettable Fire.* Widely published here and abroad, her most recent poems and non-fiction appear in *Mid-Atlantic Country, Poetry Digest, Snowy Egret, Iowa Woman, Orbis,* and *New Stone Circle.* Her collection of Japaniform poetry won the Cicada Award; she is the recipient of a Poetry Society of America Prize and The Crucible Award.

DOROTHY PARKER (1893–1967)

was one of the 20th century's most legendary wits, so celebrated for her barbed remarks that, for a time, any humorous statement was attributed to her regardless of its origin. Her short stories are notable for their bittersweet cynicism and sensitivity to social cruelties; her poetry is often flippant in tone with an undercurrent of melancholy and despair. Parker wrote several volumes of poetry and short stories, theatre and book reviews, journalism, stage plays, and film scripts (including the original version of *A Star is Born*). She came to regret her reputation as a wit, believing that her concern for social issues was not taken seriously for this reason.

DEBRA PENNINGTON

is a senior associate editor of *Alaska Quarterly Review* and an Assistant Professor of English at Kodiak College, a branch of the University of Alaska Anchorage. A lifelong Alaskan, she has also taught junior and senior high school in Mountain Village and Nome, Alaska. Her poetry has recently appeared in *The Atlantic Monthly* and other publications.

HELEN PINKERTON

was born in 1927 in Butte, Montana, and now lives in Palo Alto, California. Her collections of poetry are *Error Pursued* (Cummington and Stone Wall: Iowa City, 1959), *Poems 1946–1976* (Goodman Gybbe: Huntsville, 1984), and *Bright Fictions: Poems on Works of Art* (R.L. Barth: Edgewood, Kentucky, 1994). Under her married name, Helen Trimpi, she has also published the scholarly study *Melville's Confidence Men and American Politics in the 1850s* (Archon: Hamden, 1987). She has taught literature and writing at Stanford, College of Notre Dame (Belmont, CA), University of Alberta, and Michigan State University.

D.A. PRINCE

was born in Leicestershire, England, to Welsh parents, in 1947. Her poems are widely published in magazines and in anthologies of light verse, including *The Random House Treasury of Light Verse.* She is currently working on her first collection.

SIMA RABINOWITZ

lives in Minneapolis, Minnesota. Her poetry and prose have appeared in a number of publications, and she is a regular writer for the *Hungry Mind Review*. She has received a Loft Mentor Series Award in poetry, a Loft Creative Nonfiction Award, and a 1996 Minnesota State Arts Board grant for poetry.

NAOMI RACHEL's
recent poetry and short fiction have appeared in the *Nimrod Awards Issue, Hampden Sydney Poetry Review, New Virginia Review, Outerbridge, Denver Quarterly,* and *The Hawaii Review*. A chapbook, *The Temptation of Extinction,* was published by Senex Press, San Francisco. She teaches Creative Writing and Women's Literature at the University of Colorado.

SUSAN BLACKWELL RAMSEY
was born in Detroit, Michigan, in 1950. She currently lives in Kalamazoo with her husband and three children and works for the only bookstore in Kalamazoo older than she is. Her poetry has appeared in *Poetry Motel* and *The Atlanta Review,* among other publications.

ELISAVIETTA RITCHIE's
books include *Flying Time: Stories & Half-Stories, The Arc of the Storm, Elegy for the Other Woman: New & Selected Terribly Female Poems, Tightening the Circle Over Eel County* (winner of the Great Lakes Colleges Association's 1975-76 "New Writer's Award"), and *Raking the Snow* (winner of the 1981-82 Washington Writer's Publishing House competition). She also edited *The Dolphin's Arc: Endangered Creatures of the Sea*.

MARGARET ROGERS
is a Yorkshire-woman, born, bred, and educated (with an M.A. in English) in Sheffield, England. The widow of an architect and mother of one daughter, she now lives alone, paints, and writes poetry.

VERNA SAFRAN
teaches adult education classes in the Center for Professional Development at Florida State University. She also writes articles on art and politics for local and national publications and is editor of *The Seven Hills Fiction Review* for the Tallahassee Writers Association. Her poetry has appeared in numerous publications; her chapbooks include *Womanstages* (HER Press, Gretna, LA), *Stepping Stones* and *Love Is the Answer; What Was the Question?* (both by Fruit Tree Press, Ocala, FL).

SAPPHO (fl. c. 610–c. 580 B.C.)
was the greatest lyric poet of Western antiquity. Most of her poems are vernacular, not literary, in tone, with a direct and precise use of language. They include many love poems written to women friends; several others address her daughter, Kleis. In the Greek and Roman worlds, poets frequently knew her ten books of poetry by

heart. In the 11th century A.D., the church undertook a systematic destruction of her work, and her books were publicly burned in Rome and Constantinople. The few writings that survive, mostly fragments of poems, were preserved in quotations by other ancient authors or found in later papyrus discoveries.

JOANNE SELTZER
was born in Detroit and now makes her home in upstate New York. In addition to poetry, she has published short fiction and literary essays. Her work appears regularly in small press magazines and in many anthologies, including *Women of the 14th Moon, Women Speak to God: The Prayers and Poems of Jewish Women,* and the award-winning *When I Am an Old Woman I Shall Wear Purple.* She has also published three poetry chapbooks.

ANNE SEXTON (1928-1974)
published numerous volumes of poetry; her work is noted for its intensity of feeling and its openness in revealing personal details, particularly her struggles with mental illness. Associated with the Confessionalist movement (she studied with Snodgrass and Lowell and was acquainted with Plath), Sexton was one of the first women poets to write candidly on such subjects as menstruation and abortion. The recipient of many grants, honors, and awards for poetry, she also wrote a play, *Mercy Street,* that had a brief run in New York City. She died by suicide.

GRACE SIMPSON
is a former English and Journalism teacher who lives in Hampden-Sydney, Virginia. Her poems have appeared in such journals as *Negative Capability, Southern Poetry Review, Snake Nation Review, Cincinnati Poetry Review, Zone 3,* and *The Formalist.*

STEVIE SMITH (1902–1971)
was raised by her mother and aunt in "a house of female habitation," her father having deserted the family. While working on her poetry and novels, she supported herself as a secretary and by writing book reviews. In 1953 a physical and emotional breakdown brought about her retirement from office work. Smith was the author of three novels, several books of poetry illustrated with her own distinctive drawings, essays, and radio plays. In later life she found considerable success reading her poems on the radio and in person; Glenda Jackson, who portrayed the poet on stage and film, remembered her as such a charismatic performer that Jackson was reluctant to follow her onstage. Admirers of Smith's poetry included Ogden Nash, who wrote a poem in her honor, Robert Lowell, and Sylvia Plath.

JUDITH SORNBERGER's
poetry collection *Open Heart* was published by Calyx Books in 1993; her chapbook

of poems, *Judith Beheading Holofernes,* appeared in the same year from Talent House Press. Her poems have appeared in *Prairie Schooner, Calyx, Puerto del Sol,* and *West Branch.* She is an associate professor of English and Women's Studies at Mansfield University in the mountains of north-central Pennsylvania. Her muse is a salt-and-pepper cockapoo named Roxy.

LAUREL SPEER

has been publishing poetry, fiction, and essays in small press and literary magazines for over thirty years. She has "always had a female hawk's eye out for the male literary icons." Her latest publications are a poem pamphlet, *Rebecca at the Port Authority,* and a prose pamphlet, *Blood & Puppets.* She is also a contributing editor for *Small Press Review.*

A.E. STALLINGS

studied Classics at the University of Georgia and at Oxford. Her work appears in *The Atlanta Review, The Beloit Poetry Journal, Classical Outlook, Hellas, The Formalist, Light, The Lyric, Poetry,* and *Snake Nation Review,* and has been anthologized in *The Best American Poetry 1994* and *Orpheus & Co.*

STEPHANIE STRICKLAND

has published three full-length poetry collections: *Give the Body Back* (University of Missouri Press, 1991), *The Red Virgin: A Poem of Simone Weil* (University of Wisconsin Press, 1993), and *True North* (University of Notre Dame Press, 1996). *The Red Virgin* was a winner of the Brittingham Prize, and *True North* was a recipient of the Sandeen Poetry Prize and the PSA's Di Castagnola Prize. Her poetry has received many other awards and has appeared in numerous magazines, including *The Paris Review, The Kenyon Review, Prairie Schooner,* and *Ploughshares.*

SARA TEASDALE (1884–1933)

was the author of six books of poetry, winning the Pulitzer Prize for *Love Songs* in 1918. Her early poems, for which she is best known, are brief, personal lyrics using simple forms, frequently on the subject of feminine love; her later work tends to be darker and more austere. Teasdale was courted by the poet Vachel Lindsay—a romance encouraged by her friend Harriet Monroe, founder of *Poetry*—but rejected him and married a businessman, whom she later divorced. Her last years were spent in seclusion and she died by suicide.

LEE UPTON's

third book of poetry, *Approximate Darling,* was published in 1996 by the University of Georgia Press. Her second book of criticism, *Obsession and Release: Rereading the Poetry of Louise Bogan,* appeared in the same year from Bucknell University Press.

LENORE BAELI WANG's
work has appeared in *Calyx, Footwork: The Paterson Literary Review, Exit 13, Sinister Wisdom, Sisters Today,* and other magazines. Malafemmina Press published her chapbook, *Born in the Year of the Pink Sink.* She teaches at Rider University and was the judge for the 1995 Wyoming Writer's Poetry Competition.

CAROLYN WELLS (1869–1942)
was a popular writer and editor of humorous poetry in the early 20th century. Books written or edited by her included *At the Sign of the Sphinx, A Whimsey Anthology, An Outline of Humor, The Rest of My Life, The World's Best Humor,* and *The Book of Humorous Verse.*

KATHLEENE WEST
has published seven books of poetry and fiction, including the poetry collections *Water Witching* (Copper Canyon Press) and *The Farmer's Daughter* (Sandhills Press). Her work has appeared in *Notre Dame Review, Ploughshares, Prairie Schooner, Triquarterly, The Alaska Review,* and in a previous Story Line Press anthology, *A Formal Feeling Comes: Poems in Form by Contemporary Women.*

GAIL WHITE
lives in Breaux Bridge, Louisiana, on the banks of Bayou Teche. She started writing formal poetry long before it was in fashion. Her work appears in numerous magazines, including *Light, The Formalist, Hellas,* and *The Dark Horse,* and in the anthology *A Formal Feeling Comes: Poems in Form by Contemporary Women.* A four-woman anthology is forthcoming from Singular Speech Press. She lives with her husband, Arthur, who designed their English-cottage house, and with Fat Cat and Yellow Cat, who shed a lot.

PATRICIA WILCOX
(a.k.a. E.V. Austin) has published two volumes of poems, *A Public and Private Hearth* (Bellevue Press, 1978) and *An Exile from Silence* (Alembic Press, 1981), as well as a novel, *The House by the Side of the Road* (Iris Press, 1975). Her poetry and stories have appeared in such journals as *The New Republic, Denver Quarterly, Missouri Review, The Emory University Quarterly,* and *The Epigrammatist;* her reviews and critical studies have been published in *Small Press Review, Contact II, Creeping Bent,* and *Tar River Poetry.* She is the Editor/Publisher Emeritus of Iris Press, which she founded in 1975 and ran for more than a decade. She lives with her husband, the philosophy scholar John T. Wilcox, in Binghamton, New York.

NANCY WINTERS
was born in Chicago, raised in Cleveland, Ohio, and has lived in California since

1959. She was educated at Mills College, the University of California at Berkeley, the University of Bordeaux, and San Francisco State University, where she received a B.A. in French language and literature. Her poetry has appeared in a number of periodicals, and she is the author of two chapbooks, *A Sad and Solemn Ground* and *Talking to Birds.* She served as editor of *The Epigrammatist* from 1994 to 1996 and, with R.L. Barth, has revived his press, which has concentrated on contemporary, mostly formal, American poetry.

ANITA WINTZ

was educated at Harvard and Cornell, and now lives in California with her husband. Her work has appeared in *Light, Sticks, Sparrow,* and in several anthologies. Her poetry for young readers is included in *Riddle-Me Rhymes* and *Call Down the Moon: Poems of Music.*

PHYLLIS WITTE

resides in Brooklyn and gives numerous poetry readings throughout New York City. She has been a winner of the Allen Ginsberg Poetry Series Award and the Pat Parker Memorial Award; she was also a winner and featured reader at the In Our Own Write series at the Gay and Lesbian Community Center. Her work has been published widely in magazines and anthologies. She holds an M.F.A. from Brooklyn College and teaches English at Brooklyn Tech High School.

SUSANNA E. ZEIDLER (1665?–1706?)

was the daughter of Rector Gottfried Zeidler of Fienstadt, Germany, and the sister of Johann Gottfried Zeidler. Her book of poetry, *Jungferlicher Zeitvertreiber in allerhand Gedichten (Maidenly Pastimes in Sundry Poems),* was published in 1686. Nothing more is known about her life.

Acknowledgments

Previously unpublished poems are used by permission from their authors, who retain all rights. Grateful acknowledgment for previously published work is given to the following:

Anna Akhmatova: "Lot's Wife," from *Poems* by Anna Akhmatova, translated by Lyn Coffin. Translation copyright © 1983 by Lyn Coffin. Reprinted by permission of WW Norton & Company, Inc.

Margaret Atwood: "Siren Song" and excerpts from "Circe/Mud Poems" © Margaret Atwood, 1974. Originally published in *You Are Happy,* Oxford University Press (Toronto).

Grace Bauer: "Note from the Imaginary Daughter," *Apalachee Review.*

Maxianne Berger: "Afterthought," Matrix 41 (Canada).

Judith Bishop: "The Profession," *Coast Light: An Anthology of Northern California Poets* (Coastlight Press, 1981).

Louise Bogan: "Hypocrite Swift," from *The Blue Estuaries* by Louise Bogan. Copyright © 1968 by Louise Bogan. Reprinted by permission of Farrar, Straus & Giroux, Inc.

Penny Cagan: "Winning the Prize," *Calyx.*

Kelly Cherry: "Going Down on America: The Regional Poet," *Relativity* (Louisiana State University Press, 1977); "Reading, Dreaming, Hiding," *God's Loud Hand* (Louisiana State University Press, 1993); "Lady Macbeth on the Psych Ward," *Time Out of Mind* (March Street Press, 1994); "To Catullus—Highet," "The Bride of Quietness," *Lovers and Agnostics* (Carnegie Mellon University Press, 1995).

Katharine Coles: "Donna Julia's First Letter After Juan's Departure for Cadiz" first appeared in *Shenandoah,* then in *The One Right Touch* (Ahsahta Press, 1992).

Jane Cooper: "a poem with capital letters," copyright © 1974 by Jane Cooper. Reprinted by permission of the author and Tilbury House, Publishers, from *Scaffolding: Selected Poems* 1984-93.

Wendy Cope: "John Clare," *The Dark Horse;* used by permission of the author. "Waste Land Limericks" and "A Policeman's Lot" from *Making Cocoa for Kingsley Amis,* © Wendy Cope, 1986 (Faber & Faber Ltd.); "An Argument with Wordsworth," "Variations on Belloc's 'Fatigue'," and "Tumps" from *Serious Concerns,* © Wendy Cope, 1992 (Faber & Faber Ltd.). Used by permission of Faber & Faber Ltd.

Enid Dame: "Noah's Daughter," *Tikku;* "Dina's Happy Ending," *New York Quarterly;*

"Esther," *Davka*; "Jael's Poem," *On the Road to Damascus, Maryland* (Downtown Poets, New York, 1980).

Rhina P. Espaillat: "Answering to Rilke," *Amelia*; "For Robert Frost," *The Lyric*.

Annie Finch: "Coy Mistress" first appeared in *The Formalist* and later in *A Formal Feeling Comes: Poems in Form by Contemporary Women* (Story Line Press, 1994).

Nola Garrett: "Names of Curtains," *Poet Lore*.

Julia Goldberg: "The Boys *I* Mean," *Conceptions*.

Marilyn Hacker: "Elevens" and "Riposte" from *Going Back to the River* by Marilyn Hacker (Random House). Used by permission of Marilyn Hacker.

H.D.: "Lais," "Heliodora," "Nossis," and excerpts from "Calypso" from *Collected Poems of H.D.: 1912-1944.* Copyright © 1982 by the Estate of Hilda Doolittle. Reprinted with permission of New Directions Publishing Corp.

Barbara Harr: "Walking through a Cornfield in the Middle of Winter, I Stumble over a Cow Pie and Think of the Sixties Press" used by permission of Juanita M. Harr.

Ann Hayes: "For Homer's Mosquito," *Letter at Christmas and Other Poems* (Badger Press, 1995).

Mary Holtby: "The Tyger's Reply to Blake," *How to Be Well-Versed in Poetry* (Penguin); "The Feminine 'If'" appeared in *The Spectator* (U.K.) under the pseudonym Moyra Blyth.

Erica Jong: "The Perfect Poet," from *Becoming Light* by Erica Jong. Copyright © 1961, 1962, 1971, 1973, 1975, 1977, 1979, 1981, 1983, 1987, 1991 by Erica Mann Jong. Reprinted by permission of HarperCollins Publishers, Inc.

Carolyn Kizer: "Pro Femina," "A Muse of Water," *Mermaids in the Basment* (Copper Canyon, 1984).

Yala Korwin: "Not a Voice" first appeared in *Midstream* and later in the *Anthology of Magazine Verse 1995-96*.

Joyce La Mers: "Penelope and Ulysses Settle a Domestic Dispute, *Light*; "Observation by a Formerly Rose-Lipt Maiden, *Light Year 1988-89*.

Rachel Loden: "My Night with Philip Larkin" first appeared in *B City* and later in *The Best American Poetry 1995* (Touchstone/Simon & Schuster); "On Beria's Lap," *The Florida Review*.

Barbara Loots: "Abigail," *Sparrow*.

Amy Lowell: "Astigmatism," from *Sword Blades and Poppy Seed,* © 1914, Houghton Mifflin.

Katherine McAlpine: "Ann Wishes She'd Taken a Little More Heed," "Lucasta Remains Unconvinced," "That Ghastly Night in Dover," and "Cynara Respondet," were originally published as parts of a sequence, collectively titled "The Other Side of the Story," in *The Epigrammatist*; "Reply to a Dream Song," *Sparrow*.

Phyllis McGinley: "Dido of Tunisia" and "Public Journal," from *Times Three* by Phyllis McGinley. Copyright 1932-1960 by Phyllis McGinley; Copyright 1938-42, 1944, 1958, 1959 by The Curtis Publishing Co. Used by permission of Viking Penguin, a division of Penguin Books USA Inc.

Kel Munger: "The Red-Haired Waitress," *Lynx Eye*.

Sharon Olds: "The Language of the Brag," from *Satan Says,* by Sharon Olds, © 1980. Reprinted by permission of the University of Pittsburgh Press.

June Owens: "Sonnet to Percy in Italy, from England," *Amelia*; "Promises: On a Familiar Poem by Robert Frost," *Poetry Digest*; "A Small Quarrel with T.S. Eliot," *Poetry Society of Georgia Anthology, Vol. 71*; "What I Heard," *Tirra Lirra*.

Dorothy Parker: "From a Letter from Lesbia," by Dorothy Parker, from *The Portable Dorothy Parker* by Dorothy Parker, Introduction by Brendan Gill. Copyright 1928, renewed © 1956 by Dorothy Parker. Used by permission of Viking Penguin Books USA Inc.

Debra Pennington, "Adam's Curse Revisited," *Hellas*.

Helen Pinkerton, "On Gari Melcher's *Writing* (1905) in the Los Angeles County Museum," *Bright Fictions: Poems on Works of Art* (R.L. Barth, 1994).

Naomi Rachel: "Mark Strand," *Marilyn Magazine*; "I Ask Myself If This is the Start of a Prose Poem," *Writ Magazine*.

Muriel Rukeyser: "Myth," by Muriel Rukeyser, from *A Muriel Rukeyser Reader,* 1994, WW Norton, New York City. © William Rukeyser.

Anne Sexton: "To a Friend Whose Work Has Come to Triumph," from *All My Pretty Ones,* by Anne Sexton. Copyright © 1962 by Anne Sexton, © renewed 1990 by Linda G. Sexton. Reprinted by permission of Houghton Mifflin Company. All rights reserved.

Grace Simpson: "The Daughters of Oedipus": *The Formalist*.

Stevie Smith: "The Lads of the Village" by Stevie Smith, from *Collected Poems of Stevie Smith,* copyright © 1972 by Stevie Smith. Reprinted by permission of New Directions Publishing Corp.

Laurel Speer: "Milton's Women with Memories More than 300 Years Old" was first published in *Evil* (Bogg Publications, 1993); "Walking a Lobster with Blake along Speedway," *Lynx Eye*; "Mary's Present," *Prism International*; "Reason, My Dear Maria, Brings Us to Proximity," *Coal City Review*.

A.E. Stallings: "The Wife of the Man of Many Wiles," "Eurydice Reveals Her Strength," "Arachne Gives Thanks to Athena," *The Beloit Poetry Journal*; "Daphne," *Classical Association News* (U.K.); "A Likely Story," *The Classical Outlook*.

Sara Teasdale: "Beatrice," reprinted with the permission of Simon & Schuster, from *Collected Poems of Sara Teasdale* (New York, Macmillan, 1937).

Lee Upton: "Gertrude to Hamlet," "Edward Lear," *Approximate Darling* (University of Georgia Press, 1996).

Kathleene West: "Pantoum to a Bearded Muse on Lines by Robert Graves," *The Farmer's Daughter* (Sandhills Press, 1988).

Gail White: "Medea's Soliloquy," *Plains Poetry Journal*; "Corinna's Not Going A-Maying," "Rose Aylmer's Cousin," "The Shropshire Lad's Fiancee," The Formalist; "Walt Whitman Encounters the Cosmos with the Cats of New York," *Eclectic Literary Forum* (ELF).

Patricia Wilcox: "Three-Part Invention for Celan," *Denver Quarterly*.

Bibliography

In addition to individual poetry collections, the following books were consulted in assembling the poems in this volume, notes to the poems, and biographical information.

The Admirable Lady Mary, Lewis Gibbs (Morrow, 1945)

Anne Sexton, Diane Wood Middlebrook (Houghton Mifflin, 1991)

An Anthology of Light Verse, ed. Louis Kronenberger (Modern Library, 1935)

The Book of Humorous Verse, ed. Carolyn Wells (Garden City Publishing Company, 1936)

A Book of Women Poets from Antiquity to Now, ed. Aliki Barnstone and Willis Barnstone (Schocken Books, 1992)

Bulfinch's Mythology, Edmund Fuller (Dell, 1962)

Classic Myths in English Literature and in Art, Charles Mills Gayley (Ginn and Company, 1939)

The Continental Edition of World Masterpieces (W.W. Norton, 1974)

Dictionary of the Bible, ed. James Hastings (Scribner's, 1920)

Eighteenth Century Women Poets, ed. Roger Lonsdale (Oxford University Press, 1990)

The Encyclopedia Britannica (15th Edition, 1978)

English Poets of the Eighteenth Century, ed. Cecil A. Moore (Henry Holt, 1935)

A Formal Feeling Comes: Poems in Form by Contemporary Women, ed. Annie Finch (Story Line Press, 1994)

Herself Defined: The Poet H.D. and Her World, Barbara Guest (Doubleday, 1984)

Keepers of the Flame: Literary Estates and the Rise of Biography, Ian Hamilton (Hutchinson, 1992)

The LeGallienne Book of American Verse, ed. Richard LeGallienne (Boni & Liveright, 1925)

Mythology, Edith Hamilton (New American Library, 1961)

The Norton Anthology of English Literature, Third Edition (W.W. Norton, 1975)

The Norton Book of Classical Literature, ed. Bernard Knox (W.W. Norton, 1994)

Onward and Upward: A Biography of Katharine S. White, Linda H. Davis (Fromm International Publishing Company, 1989)

The Oxford Book of Short Poems, ed. P.J. Kavanagh and James Michie (Oxford University Press, 1985)

Roman Poets of the Early Empire, ed. A.J. Boyle and J.P. Sullivan (Penguin, 1991)

Stevie, Jack Barbera and William McBrien (Oxford University Press, 1985)

The Top 500 Poems, ed. William Harmon (Columbia University Press, 1992)

When God Was a Woman, Merlin Stone (Dorset Press, 1990)

The White Goddess, Robert Graves (Noonday Press, 1990)

(Woman) Writer, Joyce Carol Oates (E.P. Dutton, 1988)

The Wordsworth Dictionary of Classical and Literary Allusion, Abraham H. Lass, David Kiremidjian, and Ruth M. Goldstein (Wordsworth Editions Ltd., 1994)

You Might as Well Live: The Life and Times of Dorothy Parker, John Keats (Simon and Schuster, 1970)

Index of Titles and First Lines

Index of Authors and Translators

Index of Male Poets Addressed